Blitz Your Book to a Best Seller 21st Century

Compiled by

Joyce Spizer Foy & Virginia Clark

Blitz Your Book to a Best Seller 21st Century
Copyright © 2016 Joyce Foy and Virginia Clark
Library of Congress: 1-3778711681

Requests for information should be addressed to:
A Vegas Publisher, LLC
www.avegaspublisher.com
avegaspubisher@yahoo.com

First Edition: 2016

Cover and interior design by: Tugboat Design

*This book is dedicated to all the aspiring writers
who dream about the day when they hold
their book in their arms – at last.
I applaud your commitment to your story,
your dedicated hard work, and unending enthusiasm.
May you all have best sellers.*

DISCLAIMER

As with any publication that contains names, addresses, telephone numbers, and internet information, you must always investigate its accuracy. This world moves at the speed of technology, and the only constant in this life is change.

Although exhaustive efforts for all sources have been researched to ensure the accuracy and completeness of the information contained herein at the time of publication, we assume no responsibility for errors, inaccuracies, omissions, or any other inconsistency herein. People move, businesses close, philosophies change. That's life. Any perceived slights against people or organizations are unintentional.

No one paid to be included. There are so many more resources not listed. We encourage you to conduct your own investigation.

The authors do not endorse, recommend, or support any sources listed herein, nor can they validate their competence, or credibility. Readers should consult their loved ones, accountant, publicist, agent, editor, attorney, or other outside professional sources, including their own good judgment before engaging in, supporting, or funding any ventures listed in this book.

TABLE OF CONTENTS

INTRODUCTION

Congratulations!

You've written a book. After numerous revisions and many rejections, you've signed a contract with a major house, a small independent press, or maybe you contacted a printer with an eye toward self-publishing.

You may think you can kick back and wait for those royalty checks. Browse *Publishers Weekly* for those glowing reviews. Did Kimmel, Fallon, or Ellen call to book you on the talk-show circuit?

If you think your participation in this project is over when you have your book in hand, consider this. All those hours writing, proofreading, and making changes were infinitesimal components of becoming an author and constitute about 10% of your total work.

How are you going to find me to buy your book? Marketing and promotion are the other 90%. Who is going to sell that first edition? You are.

Hey, wait just a minute, you're thinking. My publisher promised to do all the marketing. They're orchestrating my book tours. They'll handle all the publicity. I'm the author.

Wrong. You're the information system, the conductor who will orchestrate your success or failure. Marketing and promoting are the most important phases of your work and begin the moment you decide to write one word of your book.

Where do you begin? If you have some concept or not the vaguest idea, this book has been written with you in mind. It represents the best of all writing worlds, covering the processes you should know before launching your book.

During Foy's debut book tour, she made a million mistakes, scored numerous successes, and picked up a world of pointers along the way. This guide is filled with those experiences – the good, the bad, and the ugly.

You may think your book is the grandest product of all times. A surefire hit. A blockbuster. A classic that will live forever. Good. You've mastered the first step: believing in your product.

This book will help you with the next step – attracting buyers for your product.

So, grab that highlighter, and let's go to work.

CHAPTER 1

It's Never Too Early to Plan

You're an author. You followed all the primary writing rules. Your work appears professional on paper. You read lots of "how-to" books and know everything about the writer's bible, the *Literary Market Place* also known as the *LMP*. http://www.literarymarketplace.com/lmp/us/index_us.asp

You subscribe to and/or diligently read several magazines that have their pulse on the publishing industry: i.e., *Publishers Weekly*, PO Box 16957, North Hollywood, CA 91615-6957, http://subs.publishersweekly.com/footer/contact/ and *Writer's Digest,* http://www.writersdigest.com/contact-us

You mastered your craft at creative writing classes and worked with a local critique group to make the book the best work it can be. You networked the industry's pulse at writers' conferences, joined local, regional, national, and world-wide writing organizations, and told all your friends and family about your project.

First, determine if you need an agent or whether the houses you query require an agent. Finding the right agent is like a marriage. Some work, some don't. Try to select one who is a member of the Association of Artist's Representatives to best protect you and your work. If you found one you're thinking about, check them out on internet sites like:

Association of Artist's Representatives-
http://aaronline.org/page-1758521

Writer Beware-
http://www.sfwa.org/2010/02/beware-of-fake-awards/

Another resource is-
http://invirtuo.cc/prededitors/peals.htm

Google Groups-
https://groups.google.com/forum/#!overview

Publisher's Marketplace-
http://www.publishersmarketplace.com

Agent Query-
http://www.agentquery.com

To find a publisher, newspaper, magazine, agent, or almost anything else related to publishing? In addition to the *LMP* tome in the library and on the internet, check out this site: http://everyonewhosanyone.com

You found the right agent and/or publisher for Book #1. Think you're headed for that dark solitary room to write the sequel? Wait a minute. Who's going to sell the first one? Unless you're fortunate enough to be a major celebrity or some-one with spontaneous name recognition, have an unlimited budget, and a full-time publicist—Stephen King can phone his publicity in, but you can't.

First, you must establish a depth of knowledge in market-ing your genre. That takes a lot of research. It isn't necessary to know everything, but research puts you on the leading edge of expertise. After all, your book will compete with 55,000 to 65,000 others that are published at the same time by the top 5 houses. And those numbers don't include the self-published books coming out every day. Ideally, the business and marketing plans should be developed a year to eighteen months before publication. Two weeks before the book is in your hands is too late to catch the "gold ring".

The success of any book depends on a business and marketing plan, a realistic financial budget, and a book promotion time-line. Remember, a plan is simply that. Flexibility and experimentation are key elements to its success. Some ideas will work for certain authors and genre; other concepts fail miserably. Books, like first-run motion pictures, have short lives, often less than ninety days.

The Business Plan

Answer these basic questions:
- Who will buy my book? Define your audience.
- How do I position myself in the market to guarantee sales?
- How do I create a desire for my work?
- How do I sustain the sales over a period of time?

Of course, your friends and family will buy one. That's a myth. They've supported you throughout all the long suffering of writing and getting published. They'll expect an autographed first edition for free.

Bookstore signings are passé. Only the local store near you

will book you, and only if your publisher allows for returns and offers them a 55% discount. After signing at the local bookstores, where else is there? Social media has arrived. The old ways don't work. This book helps you identify the target markets and potentially free opportunities to get you and your book known.

Positioning yourself in the market to guarantee sales take a lot of creativity. It means catching the season if it's a holiday book. If the novel is about mothers and daughters, posture a spring release to coincide with Mother's Day. If the book is about an illness, like kidney disease; contact the National Kidney Foundation. When are their Special Olympics held? When is Organ Donor Month? National Kidney Week? Use your genre, your career, and the book's theme to develop other markets that will sell for you.

HINT: Living in today's publishing environment brings unique challenges. In my small community, four months before speaking to 2,000 women, I approached the manager of a chain store and asked him to order my book. He ordered three copies. Literally, I sold my inventory from the trunk of the car.

A few months later, I approached the store manager again. I was a keynote speaker for another conference that anticipated over four hundred attendees. The manager referred me to their "regional supervisor" with my dilemma. The store ordered three copies.

While the "perennial" authors mean sure sales

for bookstores, the mid-list, and first-time authors struggle. But don't be discouraged. Create your own alternative and unique markets.

I found a small independent book store that had a great location, constant foot traffic, and advertises regularly. I introduced myself to the owner as a local author who needed someone to carry and hand-sell my book. She's sold thousands to date.

It's a win-win for us both. When I speak, her store is the one I advertise. She receives free advertising and new customers from me. As a bonus, she has autographed first editions on display at the counter and in the genre area. A mid-list publisher or small press book can't buy that counter, end dump, or visible book space at the chains.

The lesson is: sometimes you have to work outside the box. When you can't accomplish things in a direct way, move outside the box, and develop your own distribution path.

Create a desire for this work by hyping it everywhere you go, to everyone you meet. Develop "sound bytes" that peak curiosity in others. A "sound byte" is the head-turning, gasping, breath-catching hook that grabs the reader's attention.

HINT: The sound byte for my debut novel, *The Cop was White as Snow* was, "I saw my first dead body when I was twenty-one-years-old."

A darling octogenarian once told me, "I don't know if I have a story or not. I was… (insert name of powerful Hollywood producer of the 1950's) …mistress for twenty-three years." Now that's a sound byte.

Make the listener/reader beg for more. Write a freelance article with excerpts. Make an announcement about this work. Create your own press release. A list of great sources otherwise overlooked can be found throughout this book.

HINT: I'm often asked the question, "How much time do *you* spend marketing?"

"From the time I get up every morning until the last light is turned out at bedtime," is my answer.

Sell. Sell. Sell.

Develop a series of speaking engagements. Attend conferences as a panelist, moderator, or keynote speaker. Join speaker bureaus, develop lecture programs and teach creative writing. Libraries often have writing groups as do the major chains. And don't overlook the book clubs: the independent ones and at the senior centers.

Become an expert in your field. That will get you invited on a free cruise for your presentation. Think free trips to spas that often need an interesting speaker to offset that soy burger their clients ate for dinner. Writer's retreats are another opportunity for a free vacation in remote, beautiful areas. Start your own conference and invite all your expert friends.

You are now the expert on your body of work. There are no limitations to the exposure you can receive when you're positioned correctly in the market.

If your budget allows, and your book's message is so unique—advertise in *Radio-TV Interview Report, Spec Marketplace,* and contact all national television talk shows.

- *Radio-TV Interview Report*
  Bradley Communications Corporation
  http://reporterconnection.com/
  and http://steveharrison.com
- *Spec Script Marketplace*
  (they also advertise scripts)
  http://nofilmschool.com

Want to know how to reach *The View, The Talk, Wendy Williams, Dr. Phil?* For the latest in up-to-date information on booking everything from major network talk shows, regional and local talk shows, and the more obscure media markets, you might subscribe to John Kremer's *Book Marketing Updates.* Published monthly by Open Horizons, http://www.bookmarket.com/openhorizons.htm

The only limitations you face are time, money, and the energy you are willing to expend to make your project successful.

The Marketing Plan

Your marketing plan should be:
- Aggressive—months before the publication date
- Intensive—during launch

- Steady—to stay in the forefront as new books try to bump your product off the shelf

Focus on developing a network of contacts like bookstores and libraries that will vigorously promote your work. Don't overlook resources in cities where you currently live and work, and all others since your birth.

Pay particular attention to schools you attend.

Schoolmates read, they buy books, and they'll either love or hate the concept that you're successful. Spread the word. Discover conferences that promote mid-list authors and encourage your participation. Maintain a flexible plan, and don't be bashful about eliminating ideas that bomb.

During this time, your author *persona* is blossoming. Cultivate your speaking style and sound bytes. These are critical when greeting potential customers and encouraging them to buy your book. Try, "I'm a guide dog instructor." Or, "My father was a cat-burglar."

Think you're trying to sell the first book?

Yes, of course, you are. In reality, you're developing those repeat customers and finding fans who'll carry the message to others. The key to bringing your novel to the attention of the world is networking and finding that special something that culls your book from the herd of average stories. Force readers to take notice.

The time frame from contract—to print—to the public is a major source of frustration and mystery for most authors. Don't let this discourage you. This book is designed to walk you through the learning process.

Book Awards

Book awards are often overlooked by publishing houses and authors alike. The large houses say awards don't sell books, because, by the time the awards are given, the shelf life of your book is over at the large chains. It does, however, enhance your value as an author when contracting for future books. For the small and independent presses that keep your book on the shelves longer, awards do matter.

By genre, you will find all the award information, including guidelines, deadlines, and committees listed in magazines, newsletters, the internet chat clubs and blogs, organizations you join, and the all-important *Literary Market Place (LMP)*. You may need to nominate the book yourself. Others have— don't be shy. Here are the more popular ones:

AI of P: The Children's Science Writing Award in Physics and Astronomy awarded by the American Institute of Physics, One Physics Ellipse, College Park, MD 20740-3843. (301) 209-3100. info@aip.org or http://www.aip.org

ALA, also known as the American Library Association, presents the Denali Press Award recognizing the best minority and ethnic reference books. 50 E. Huron Street, Chicago, IL 60611-2795; (800) 545-2433, http://www.ala.org/editions

American Book Awards—known as the ABA Awards for fiction and nonfiction, Before Columbus Foundation, The Raymond House, 655 13th Street, Suite 302, Oakland,

CA 94612; (510)268-9775, http://www.literatureawards.
com/americanbook awards.htm or beforecolumbusfoun-
dation@gmail.com

American Booksellers Book of the Year-Children and adult
novels, http://www.bookweb.org

Benjamin Franklin Book Awards—small press titles. PMA,
the Independent Book Publishers Association,
http://ibpabenjaminfranklinawards.com/

Best Cookbook of the Year—also known as the James Beard
Foundation Book Award and formerly known as the
R. T. French Tastemaker Award. For the cooks in your
home contact The James Beard Foundation Awards,
http://www.jamesbeard.org/awards

Bookbuilders West Book Show Awards recognizes book
designers and producers http://pubpronetwork.org/
book-show/

California Writers Club—six category contest for unpub-
lished material sponsored by various CWC branches.
http://calwriters.org/

ECPA Awards—acknowledges 20 Christian book publishers
a year. Contact Evangelical Christian Publishers Association, http://www.ecpa.org/?page=cba 1 overview

Ernest Hemingway Foundation/PEN Award for First
Fiction—presents the PEN Award for First Fiction

in literary excellence. http://www.pen-ne.org/
hemingway-foundationpen-award

Gold Ink Awards—offers 21 category winners.
https://www.goldink.com/

Heartland Prizes—mid-west fiction and nonfiction. Contact
Chicago Tribune Heartland Prize

Hollywood Book Festival—offers awards in many categories
annually. They are sponsored by Final Draft Scriptware,
Imagic, and Shopper Shuttle. http://www.writermag.
com/contests/hollywood-book-festival/

Hugo Award—science fiction sponsored by
World Science-Fiction Society at
http://www.thehugoawards.org/

IRWIN awards—are given annually by the Book Publishers of
Southern California to their members. But, WOW, their
directory is a mailing list you would die for and well
worth the price of membership and networking. -
http://www.bookpublicists.org/pages/irwin_awards.asp

Nebula Award—science fiction and fantasy are sponsored
by the Science Fiction and Fantasy Writers of America.
Contact them at https://www.sfwa.org/nebula-awards/

IACP Cookbook Awards—honoring the best of food and bever-
age books. International Association of Culinary Professionals, at https://www.iacp.com/award/more/cookbook

LMP (Literary Market Place) Awards—has ten annual awards. R. R. Bowker LLC (also PubEasy, Pubnet), http://www.bowker.com/

The Poetry Foundation also offers prizes for Poetry. http://www.poetryfoundation.org/poetrymagazine/prizes

Pinnacle Book Achievement Awards and NABE Memberships - Contact http://www.bookmarketingprofits.com/PinnacleAwardsEntryForm.html

NCCJ Mass Media Awards—for the best book on human relations. Contact The National Conference for Community and Justice – diversity@nccj.org

National Book Critics Circle Book Awards—selects awards in six categories: Fiction, General Nonfiction, Biography, Autobiography, Poetry, and Criticism. Contact http://bookcritics.org/awards

National Jewish Book Awards—recognizes twenty novels each year. Contact: http://www.jewishbookcouncil.org/awards/national-jewish-book-award.html

Newbery Medal—also known as the John Newbery Medal for children's books is offered by the American Library Association, c/o The Association for Library Service to Children, http://www.ala.org/alsc/awardsgrants/bookmedia/newberymedal/newberymedal

Nobel Prize—for literature. http://www.nobelprize.org/nobel_prizes/literature/laureates/

PIA/GATF Graphic Arts Awards—is a design award. Printing Industries of America/Graphic Arts Technical Foundation, - http://www.printing.org

Pulitzer Prize—in the fields of biography, fiction, nonfiction, and poetry. Review submission guidelines. http://www.pulitzer.org/awards/2016

The Pushcart Prize—recognizes short stories, poetry, and essays. http://www.pushcartprize.com/

Spur Awards—formerly the Golden Spur Awards for ride 'em cowboy fiction and documentary novels. Contact Western Writers of America - http://westernwriters.org/spur-awards/

Violet Crown Book Awards and Teddy Children's Book Awards—to honor outstanding published books written by members. Contact the Writers' League of Texas, http://www.writersleague.org/112/Book-Awards-Contest

Writer's Digest Magazine—sponsors several awards throughout the year, including the Best Self-Published Award. Address submissions to http://www.writersdigest.com/writers-digest-competitions/self-published-book-awards

As you join organizations within your genre, you'll be introduced to specialty awards. The mystery genre, for example, offers top recognition including the Edgar, Agatha, Hammett, Shamus, Nero Wolfe, the Barry, and the Anthony. *St. Martin's Press* has the Best Mystery Award with cash and a publishing and promotional contract. http://awards.omnimystery.com/mystery-awards-smp-private-eye.html

When you win—and you will, create embossed stickers promoting this award if the publisher doesn't.

In this extremely competitive publishing industry, your work will need to stand out in the crowd. Marketing is developing and retaining long-term relationships. It's that "edge" you must nurture to succeed.

Find seminars on marketing. There are two outstanding groups in this area:

MEGA Book Marketing University—if you've ever wanted to write a book...if you have a great idea for a book...or if you're already published and simply want to sell more books, attend this three-day event... bookmarket.com and: http://writing.shawguides.com/MegaBookMarketingUniversity

Fred Pryor Seminars/Career Track is another fine organization that offers a variety of presentations. Pryor has a large selection of books, both audio, and video, to help people improve skills. http://www.pryor.com

Your work will have a greater survival rate it if it's a series. Based on the theme of your work, align yourself with major organizations or businesses. Look at the cottage industry that the Canfield-Hansen group spawned with *Chicken Soup*. For example, they have a contract with IAMS, a major pet food manufacturer, to package their *Chicken Soup for the Pet Lover's Soul* with pet food. With a vitamin and herb organization, they offer a copy of *Chicken Soup for the Enriching Soul* as a value-added product. Think beyond the box. Create a box like no other.

Set a Realistic Promotional Budget

So your publisher has promised an all-out promotional campaign that will make your book a blockbuster. Some houses will follow through; others will fall far short of your expectations. One big publisher provided only one radio interview for their author. Ah, that author was me.

The reality is that most publishers will spend more money on the printing of the book than they will on promotion. A national publisher will spend about $1,200 on a mid-list author, one who is not well-known in literary circles, or whose book is not destined to be a best-seller.

A regional or small press publisher may merely send out a few review copies and print a notice of your book in a catalog or two. Maybe they'll list you on Amazon.com. Maybe they have a distributor. Those are the cold hard facts.

Since you're dedicated to selling the first book and producing more, the budget you develop will drive the plan to succeed. As in every business, it takes money to make money.

Develop a separate budget and bank account for your out-of-pocket dollars/expenses that allow you to:

- Travel
- Produce advertising material

- Generate speaking engagements
- Pay telephone bills and copies
- Schedule and attending signings
- Host a website and other social media memberships for business

Include the set-up costs for your office and all equipment. Don't overlook maintenance, obsolescence, and replacement. Spend advertising dollars to create impressive press kits with professional photographs, handouts, and brochures. Those budget dollars may also include the hiring of a professional publicist.

If your novel sells nationwide, budget for:
- Travel expenses, including air
- Rental car, tolls, and parking
- Telephone calls
- Meals

A significant amount of the budget is allocated to advertising materials and promotion. Budget on a yearly basis, broken into months, and even days.

When speaking to groups, if no honorarium is offered, ask them to reimburse all or part of your travel expenses. Make speaking fees flexible to fit the size of the group.

HINT: Use a credit card that generates Frequent Flyer miles. Save those miles for the longest trip to the biggest conference and go in style.

In 1970, at the Third Annual Clarion Science Fiction Workshop in Clarion, Pennsylvania, Harlan Ellison, a noted short story author, told a spell-bound audience, "Don't ever, ever give your work away. If you do, you'll be typecast as an amateur, and nobody will ever want to pay you."

Almost thirty years later, he told eager writers at the Palm Springs Writers Conference, "Don't give it away. You're a business. Charge for it. When you're not speaking, you're not writing. And when you're not writing, you aren't earning money."

As I shook my head and smiled, he looked me square in the eyes and asked, "Spizer. Are you giving it away again?"

So I "charged" forth. Shortly after the conference, I was invited to speak at a private women's club. I quoted them a $200 honorarium. The organizer said they didn't have that much money in their budget. She expected 100 to attend, so I suggested she add two dollars to the cost of each ticket that included dinner. Be creative. Make it a win-win.

When speaking in small towns, ask the organizer for transportation to and from the airport to save on rental car costs. In one California community, the hostess was the chief of police, and I rode in a patrol unit.

Often the hostess will invite friends in for potluck dinners to "Meet the Author." Books sell over dessert and coffee.

Budgeting begins while negotiating your publishing contract. Ask for the author's free copies, plus the freedom to purchase copies at a deeply discounted price for marketing and sales use. No matter what the contract calls for, remember you can negotiate anything. When asking for more, be ready to give solid evidence that it's in the best interest of the book and the publisher.

Those copies don't count toward your royalties. However,

if that's a concern, find a local store. Ask them to order your books and sell them to you at their cost. This way they sell books, and you receive royalties. You'll buy inexpensive copies that you, in turn, sell at full price. Another win-win.

The average cost you'll pay for these promotional books is generally the same price as bookstores pay: 40% to 55% off the list price. How many copies you ultimately use for promotion, and how many you sell is up to you.

There are many items to consider in your marketing and promotional budget. These are basics when calculating start-up costs:

- Promotional materials
- Printing
- Postage and office supplies
- Travel
- Office maintenance
- State-of-the-art equipment
- Telephone and the internet

Depending on your lifestyle, you may have to factor in other expenses. Do you need to provide for child care or for boarding Fido or Miss Kitty? Take into consideration all the provisions you must make before you embark on the promotional tour.

Let's talk about the dreaded two words we hate to hear: income taxes. Sometimes it isn't what you make, but what the IRS lets you keep, that's important. Whether you freelance, write novels, and/or teach, good record-keeping is the edge to increasing your share of the bucks.

Establish an author banking account. This simplifies checks written, and if you use a software accounting program, makes the year-end calculating as simple as a click on the screen.

If checks are written manually and you're not too computer savvy, it's best to purchase bookkeeping ledgers. One for income and one for expenses. Income includes book sales, royalty checks, and honorarium, plus any additional "value-added" product you market. But with online banking, record keeping is quite easy when checks are coded properly.

Deductible expenses may include:

- Accounting fees
- Automobile expenses
- Conference, workshop, and seminars
- Critique or reading fees, dues to professional organizations
- Equipment purchase, depreciation, and maintenance
- Insurance
- Legal Fees
- Office expenses and supplies
- Postage, manuscript boxes, and large sized envelopes
- Printing and copy costs
- Secretarial services, including typing and copying
- Taxes
- Travel and entertainment
- Utilities
- Membership and website fees

Remember to keep an accurate record of all these expenses, especially travel. Most office supply stores carry mileage and expenditure logs to accurately record these costs. Some items will be fully tax deductible. A CPA or tax consultant is the best person to advise you. A professional can also suggest ways of record keeping that will save hours and dollars at tax time.

For the computer savvy person, simply buy and use Neat Receipts. It's inexpensive, accepted by the IRS, and after you scan the receipts, shred them. There's no need to store more paper. At the year's end, hit the print button and send the documents to your accountant. Backup last year's data on a pen drive too to assure its safety. It's that simple.

How much money will you need to spend? Peter Lance, the author of *First Degree Burn,* spent $4,032 of his own money to produce 1,200 promotional copies of the $5.99 mystery paperback. Through September 1997, when a *Wall Street Journal* article was written about his marketing plan, he had spent $34,762 of his own money to spotlight his work among the 55,000 titles published that quarter.

Did you read about Joe Konrath? Publishers rejected nine of his comic thriller novels, but when peddling the tenth, Hyperion gave him a low six-figure advance for three of the books in 2003. Konrath spends 90% of his time and about $40,000, nearly half his annual income, marketing his books.

It's worth repeating: it takes money to make money. Although most of us don't have that kind of money to spend on promotion, a good rule of thumb is to plan on spending almost all of your royalty checks and advance. Most of these will be up-front expenses, but are often tax deductible against your income.

Establishing a Promotional Time-Line

The publication schedule drives the book's promotion. Most publishers produce a spring and fall catalog. Remember, your book will be competing with thousands of others being published during the same period of time. Unless you are fortunate enough to be a celebrity and have lots of money for marketing and promotion, you must work smarter than the others to make your book stand out.

Let's assume you're not a major author, yet. Ask your house to publish offseason, when you're not competing with block-buster authors. You'll need the edge.

Try not to get published in the last quarter of the year, because in ninety days the book will chronologically be a year old. If it's published in January, the book has twelve months to be fresh. It's a psychological thing. Think current.

The time frame between the contract and printing of the book is prime time to position your book for the market.

A bit of ingenuity on your part will help position the book for the highest market exposure.

Timing may not be everything, but it's important. Try to schedule the publication date to coincide with a significant time in history relating to the work. For instance, if the book is a biography of a major literary figure, coordinate with her or his birthday. A dessert cookbook with lots of gooey delights? Catch the Thanksgiving and Christmas seasons. A children's book featuring rabbits? Perfect for book tables before Easter.

If the setting of your latest crime thriller is a New England fall, advertising and sales plans should be in place by September when the leaves are beginning to turn. Murder at a seaside resort? Have the novel available by late May so it's the first book vacationers tuck into their travel bags.

If your life has been devastated by sorrow, do what the newspapers do for sensationalism, "catch the exploitation buzz." After the Columbine High School tragedy in April 1999, the mother of victim Cassie Bernall popped a hardback out in ninety days.

According to the July 1999, *Wall Street Journal's* article on Bernall's book, super-agent Jonathon Lazear said, "I'm marketing virtually everything you can exploit, and I mean that in a positive way." Misty Bernall's publicists and agents:

- Booked her on the network's talk show circuit
- Placed the book in mass market stores like Wal-Mart, K-Mart, and Costco
- Shopped the story around Hollywood
- Taped an inspirational video
- Excerpted the book for major magazines
- Sold book-club rights
- Created a website where teens could share feelings
- Sold European rights
- Considered setting up a charitable foundation with proceeds from the book

The Direct Marketing Association reports that the best months for promotions are in January, February, October, August, November, and September—in that order. But that doesn't mean that a book on bunny rabbits shouldn't be hopping into stores in time for Easter. Or a book on patriotism shouldn't be waving into stores in time for July 4th.

Bookstores set their Christmas promotions early and do no direct mailings after November 13th. With the holidays and the increased mail-flow, don't get lost in the seasonal rush. The next best date for promotional mailings is January 2nd.

Maybe Richard Paul Evans' *Christmas Box* will sell all year long, but that's an exception to the rules.

Getting Those All-Important Reviews

The minute your publisher sends you galley proofs to correct, plan book reviews. These professional critiques are critical to the book's success. The publisher should mail review copies at least ninety days before the official "pub date." Ask the editor/publisher for a copy of his list and verification of the date the books were mailed.

Use your personal list and send out several more. Copies may be bound or for advance review copies (ARC), AKA known as galleys. Verify, however, that the reviewers will read from galleys. To avoid duplication, double check your roster against that of the publishing house. Rubber stamp them as review copies so they won't be sold as new books.

Following is a list of the major players in the book review media. As with any address and telephone listing in a published book, always call first to verify the accuracy of the information. The publishing industry is constantly on the move. If the information is not on the internet, with one telephone call, ask for a copy of their submission guidelines, the name of the review editor for your genre, and check their address.

Send a galley to that person's attention. On the envelope write "REQUESTED MATERIAL." These two all-important words may keep you from being unceremoniously dumped on the slush pile.

Don't waste time or expense sending it Return Receipt Requested, Certified Mail, or Overnight. The package is opened in a mail room by someone who doesn't have time to read, placed in a bin for that specific editor, and later transported to the bottom of his or her slush pile.

A cover letter should accompany the galley. It must be

compelling and dramatic enough to cause the editor/reviewer to read it. Pattern the letter after your query letter—one page with lots of punch. Don't forget to mention the "pub date."

The editor/reviewer needs to know, without looking on the copyright page, how long he/she has to read and review the book before publication to give you the best possible market exposure.

Their magazines and newspapers have deadlines, too. If it's received too late, you've lost that edge.

Book Sense is a venture of the American Booksellers Association. Its unique program offers online and in-store marketing and promotion for participating independent bookstores. It's the American Booksellers Association's answer to Amazon. com and other online book retailers.

- With information gathered from an association of over 1,000 stores, *Book Sense* compiles a top ten list of recommended reads
- Bookstores can customize websites, and link with authors
- Focuses on small press releases
- Publishes *Bookselling This Week,* a newsletter about the independent marketplace
- Visit *Book Sense* at http://www.bookweb.org/btw-topics/book-sense For general questions, contact http://www.bookweb.org/american-booksellers-association
- Offers co-op advertising between the publishing house and the bookstores
- Contact *Book Sense* at ABA. 200 White Plains Road, Tarrytown, NY 10591. (800) 637-0037, (914) 591-2665. http://www.bookweb.org

General Book Reviewers

Association of College and Research Libraries is located at 50 E. Huron Street, Chicago, IL 60611-2795; (312) 280-2517 or (800) 545-2433, http://www.ala.org/acrl

Booklist—a bi-weekly publication of the American Library Association. They review 10,000 books a year. Located at 50 E. Huron Street, Chicago, IL 60611 (800) 545-2433, http://www. ala.org. Send Inquiries to: ala@ala.org.

Choice Magazine—published eleven times a year by the ACRL with more than 7,000 reviews of books and electronic media for those in higher education and is the leading review source for academic/research libraries. Contact them at 100 Riverview Center, Middletown. CT 06457. (860) 347-6933.

Deadly Pleasures Magazine—for those in the mystery genre, publishes four times a year. Contact George Easter at P. O. Box 969, Bountiful, UT 84011. (801) 299-9433. http://deadlypleasures.com

Horn Book Magazine—is published bi-monthly for all categories of children's literature. They review over 500 books a year and is the most prestigious reviewer of children's books in the United States. Librarians often make their purchases direct from Horn's reviews. It's a privilege to have your book reviewed favorably in this magazine. Contact them at 56 Roland Street, Suite 200, Boston, MA 02129; (800) 325-1170 or (617) 628-0225, info@ hbook.com http://www.hbook.com

Kirkus Review—published bi-weekly reviewing about 5,000 titles per year, pre-publication books of fiction, mysteries, sci-fi, translations, nonfiction, and children's books...no poetry, mass-market paperbacks, or children's picture books. (866) 890-8541. info@kirkusreviews.com http://www.kirkusreviews.com. They charge for reviewing your book, and there's no guarantee that you will like what they say -- but at least you're reviewed.

Library Journal—is published monthly for the nation's public library system. They annually review 7,500 books, audiobooks, videos/DVDs, databases, systems, and more, written by librarians for librarians. Send your book to them at 360 Park Avenue South, New York, New York, 10010. (646) 746-6734. Book review: http://reviews.libraryjournal.com

Publishers Weekly—the writer's trade magazine. They review over 5,000 books per year. This publication is the pulse of the publishing industry. Mark your submission attention *PW FORECASTS* and send to 360 Park Avenue South, New York, New York 10010. (646) 746-6758. http://www.publishersweekly.com

School Library Journal—publishes ten times a year corresponding with the school calendar, and reviews 3,000 books. Contact SLJ Home Office, 360 Park Avenue South, New York, NY 10010. (646) 746-6759. slj@reedbusiness.com and http://www. schoollibraryjournal.com/

State-Wide or Regional Book Reviewers

Each state or region has one or two book-review services that focus on books dealing with their specific region. Be sure to contact them for guidelines for submitting galleys or the published book. Several services include:

- Review of Texas Books, P. O. Box 10021, Beaumont, Texas 77710. (409) 880-8118
- Books of the Southwest, 201 W. Polk Street, Sabinal, Texas 78881; (830) 988-2566.
- Sul Ross University, http://www.sulross.edu
- Small Press Review, Dustbooks, P.O. Box 100, Paradise, CA 95967; (530) 877-6110, info@dustbooks.com

Newspaper and Magazine Reviewers

Begin by contacting your local newspaper and throw away papers. If your book garners a major newspaper review, that not only spells sales, it's one way to get your book title before many of the major bookstore chains.

Here are a few book review sources:

Chicago Tribune Books—a Sunday section for general interest reviews. Contact them at 435 N. Michigan Avenue, Chicago, IL 66011-4022. (312) 222-3232, FAX: (312) 222-4760. http://www.chicagotribune.com/features/booksmags/

Esquire Magazine—has over 700,000 readers. Send galleys to *Hearst Group*, 300 West 57th Street, New York, NY 10019. (212) 649-4020. esquire@hearst.com

New York Review of Books—published biweekly and reviews 1,500 novels. NYRB, 1755 Broadway, 5ᵗʰ Floor, New York, NY 10019. (212) 757-8070. http://www.nyrb@ nybooks.com

New York Times Book Review—the supplement to the Sunday edition of the *New York Sunday Times,* reviews over 4,000 books each year. For guidelines, write them at 229 West 43ʳᵈ Street, New York, NY 10036. (800) 631-2580, (212) 556-1234: books@nytimes.com or www.nytimes.com

Playboy—global monthly readership over 30 million. Send galleys to Editor, Book Review at 680 North Lake Shore Drive, Chicago, IL 60611. (312) 751-8000 http://www. playboy.com

San Francisco Chronicle Book Review—does 1,500 reviews per year in the Sunday *Chronicle.* Their address is 901 Mission Street, San Francisco, CA 94103. (415) 777-1111. www. sfchronicle.com

Time Magazine has four million readers each week makes this a worthwhile effort to get reviewed. Time-Life Building, 1271 Avenue of the Americas in Rockefeller Center, New York, NY 10020. (212) 522-1212. http://www.time.com

USA Today—has 21 downloads a week. (800) 828-0909, (703) 854-3400: editor@usatoday.com Send galleys to 7950 Jones Branch Dr, McLean, VA 22107

U.S. News and World Report—a digital-only *circulation* of millions will help your sales if you can break into this magazine. (202) 955-2000. letters@usnews.com http://www. usnews.com

Voice Literary Supplement—a monthly supplement of the *Village Voice* newspaper. 36 Cooper Square, New York, New York 10003-4846. (212) 475-3333. airnyc.org

Washington Post Book World—a supplement to the *Sunday Post* and reviews more than 2,500 books per year. 1150 15th Street, N.W., Washington, D.C. 20071. (202) 334-7502. Book critic, Jonathan Yardley (202) 334-7883.
http://www.washingtonpost.com

In addition to these publications, most states have an association of newspapers or media sources. You can obtain names and addresses of newspapers in your state or region that review books from the *LMP* or *Ulrich's International Periodical Directory*. Don't overlook specialty sources like airline magazines that often have book reviews. And not all publications review books, so don't do a statewide mailing. Be selective in those you choose.

Small Press Reviewers

As the publishing industry shrinks, small presses are gaining a larger and more respectful share of the market. Each year more than 5,000 new small publishing houses are established. If your book is being published by a small press or if you are self-publishing under your own imprint, check out these sources for reviews:

Bloomsbury Review®—a bimonthly publication featuring reviews of small press titles. 1245 E. Colfax Ave #304, Denver, CO 80218. (802)- 2238, (800) 783-3338, (303) 455-3123, info@bloomsburyreview.com
http://www.bloomsburyreview.com

Independent Publisher Magazine—a webzie reviews 100 books each posting. Part of the Jenkins Group, 1129 Woodmere #B, Traverse City, Michigan 49686. (616) 933-0445.
http://www. bookpublishing.com

Small Press Review—is the original periodical that reviews primarily literary fiction and poetry in its monthly issues. Contact at Dustbooks, P.O. Box 100, Paradise, CA 95967. (530) 877-6110 info@dustbooks.com

---

Specialty Reviewers

There are many review services for special interests and genres. Here are a few:

Black Issues Book Review—reviews 30 to 40 books bi-monthly. Troy Johnson. Troy@aalbc.com will tell you how to send galleys.

Bookviews—a syndicated column reaching newspapers across the country and the internet. They want the actual book, not the galley, and require little lead time. Editor Alan Caruba is a charter member of the National Book Critics Circle, contact him at The Caruba Organization, 28 West Third Street (Apt 1321), South Orange, NJ 07079. (973) 763-6392. http://carubaeditorialservices.blogspot.com

Catholic News Service—is a wire service covering over 180 Catholic newspapers in the United States and 40 predominately English-speaking countries. Review coordinator Richard Philbrick reviews one book a week in a column entitled *Books En Route*. The service also produces several specials: before Christmas and at the close of the school year. There's another monthly column *The Reading Room* written by Joseph R. Thomas. Contact them at 3211 Fourth Street, NE, Washington, D.C. 20017; (202) 541-3000.

New Age Retailer—a trade journal for the new-age body, mind and spirit booksellers with a circulation of over 5,500. Contact them at 2183 Alpine Way, Bellingham, WA 98226; (800) 463-9243, (360) 676-0789. https://www.retailinginsight.com/contactus

Notorious Magazine—has a circulation of 100,000 reviews 4 or 5 books per bi-monthly issue. They also interview authors. Send galleys to Eva Nagorski, Senior Editor, 37 East 28th Street, Suite 906, New York, New York 10016-7919. (212) 685-7837.

Romantic Times—a monthly book review magazine targeting the romance market. If your book is romance, this is the magazine for you. 81 Willoughby St #701, Brooklyn, New York, New York 11201. (718) 237-1097, rtinfo@rtbookreviews

Sci/Tech Book News—reviews highly technical, scientific,

and medical books. They are an ezine. 5739 NE Summer Street, Portland, OR 97218; (503) 281-9230, https://www.protoview.com

For additional book review sources, check *Literary Market Place* or *Ulrich's International Periodical Directory*. Look for those sources that review in your genre and have a good circulation. Don't face embarrassment. Locate and read several issues of those magazines or newsletters to make sure you have a match. This will increase your odds of being reviewed.

Book clubs are wonderful markets for increasing sales. Check out the *Literary Market Place* to identify clubs like Science Fiction, Doubleday, Book Club of the Month, Detective Book Club, Writer's Digest Book Club and hundreds more.

F&W Publishing operates five clubs: Decorative Arts, Graphic Designers, North Light (for fine arts and painting), Woodworkers, and Writer's Digest Book Clubs. Send your book to Kathy Kipp at 4700 E. Galbraith Road, Cincinnati, OH 45236. (513) 891-7196, http://www.fwcommunity.com

If your genre is mystery, these web links will review your book:
http://reviewingtheevidence.com
http://www.cluelass.com
http://www.crimeandclues.com
http://www.crimeculture.com
http://www.fictionforum.net
http://www.mysterybooksellers.com (that one is the link for joining the Independent Mystery Book Sellers Association that will help you hand-sell your work.)
http://www.mysteryreaders.org
http://www.stopyourekillingme.com

For general fiction, try these little known, but budding book review links:

http://www.wordmuseum.com
http://www.thebestreviews.com
http://www.curledup.com

While I'm told that 85% of all books are not sold at the big chains, don't overlook them, especially in your hometown. Now is a good time to meet the community service representative with the larger chains. Either mail your galley and some press information, a press kit, or your business card, and a flyer on the book, to their personal attention, or take a set by the store and introduce yourself.

Be sure to alert them to the book's publication date and tell them you are available for signings. This initial visit is only the first, so make it a memorable one. Be cordial and enthusiastic about your book. Answer all questions with confidence. Be sure to collect the owner or representative's card and a telephone number where they can be reached for a follow-up call.

Remember, these professionals are your links to the book-buying public, so make a good impression.

All this talk about calling strangers and scheduling meetings making you a bit nervous? You never thought of yourself as a salesperson, did you? Don't worry. Turn the page for your next journey.

CHAPTER 2

Heavens...How Can I Ever Give a Speech?

How many times to authors express their anxiety about public speaking? How many times do we answer, "Oh, yes you can do this?" And you must if you're ever going to sell a book.

You can't hide behind the computer any longer. The book will not sell itself. The world wants to see you and touch you and talk with you. You've pulled yourself away from the non-published writers. They yearn to learn how you did it. They want to do it, too. You're now an expert, and people want to hear your story. How'd you do it?

Developing your public persona is another key to your success as an author. No one can promote this work better than you.

Speaking before a group may sound daunting, even scary. But, it's easy to master the art. The secret is practice, practice, practice. And then practice some more.

Before you embark on your first speaking tour, try inviting a group of close friends to hear your presentation. Work on creating your individual sound bytes.

What works and what doesn't? Ask for critiques that will help you present yourself before strangers. Write down the things you want and need to work on.

Try the power of meditation, daily affirmations, and/or prayer. They are important to the "chi" balance of mind and body. They help with relaxation, and they open your energy with both force and humor.

If you still feel uneasy, help is at hand in your community. There are professional organizations, such as the Toastmasters, that can help even the most faint-hearted speak well in public. Most colleges and universities, both state and community, offer basic courses on public speaking. Many allow you to audit these classes.

Join your local little theater, even if you have to sew costumes or become an usher. Listen and learn. These provide excellent forums to help you learn to think on your feet.

Speak before members at a senior activity center. They're a great audience and so appreciative.

Offer a free speech to a youth club, a group of volunteers, or to church groups. Ask for feedback. Ask what they liked and how they thought you could improve. You might even sell a few books.

The following steps will guide you toward the podium with confidence, clarity, and calm. Don't strive to be just a good speaker, become a great one.

Step One: Be Prepared

Confirm your appearance date, the time, and the location in advance. The embarrassment of showing up on the wrong date, at the wrong time, or place has happened to authors in the past and will again. One bookstore moved before the signing and didn't notify the author. Bring a written introduction even though your press kit was mailed long ago. Better to have two copies of your introduction, than none, if the host misplaces your papers.

Discuss your presentation with the organizer. Make sure you have enough hand-outs for all the anticipated guests and, of course, plenty of books.

Know your audience and what they expect from your presentation. What is the demographics of the audience? Are you sharing creative writing tools, talking about your career, or inspiring others? You speak for three reasons: to inform, to entertain, and to educate.

If this is a question-and-answer program give your presenter a pre-selected list of questions that you believe the audience would like answered. If you've spoken more than once, you're already starting to hear the questions repeated. Your answers are becoming stronger and more spontaneous.

Need props? Always ask about the size of the room and what equipment is available: Microphone, overhead projector, easel, and screen. Don't wait until the last minute to need important pieces of equipment. And, when you arrive, test it. Outlets short out. Batteries die. Life happens. Be prepared. Adjust and overcome.

On presentation day, give yourself ample time to locate the site and park. Plan to arrive at least thirty to forty-five minutes early for set-up and freshen-up time.

There is nothing that makes you feel more at ease than knowing your material. The elements to success as a public speaker whether you entertain, inform, or educate, are to practice, practice, practice. That's the whole secret. Speaking in a clear, articulate voice is your goal. Write out your speech, or work from note cards. Whatever makes you feel comfortable.

Nothing takes the place of knowing your material thoroughly. However, don't try to memorize the presentation. That makes it sound wooden and stilted.

You don't have to follow the written text exactly, but at least have an outline, notes, or speech cards to cue you. They help you stay on track. Remember your time constraints, and don't abuse them. And always allow extra time in the event you're asked to remain longer. And NEVER, EVER read from your book. Trust me.

Step Two: Speak with Enthusiasm and Warmth

No one knows your book better than you do. No one has fallen in love with those characters; no one knows their feelings and motivations like you. Sell yourself, and the book will sell itself.

Now, make your audience believe in your book enough to buy it. Practice before a mirror, not only for the clarity of delivery but for the timing as well. Watch those facial expressions. Rehearse over and over again, removing the "uh," and local phrases that detract, "like, you know." Try not to look terrified, even if you are. Be sure to smile at the audience. A bright, twinkling smile, and a voice that conveys warmth will bring your audience to you and result in increased book sales.

If you're nervous, don't feel well, or have personal problems, like car trouble or a sick child—keep it to yourself. Above all, do not apologize. It won't bring the audience to your side and causes embarrassment for you, the audience, and the organizer.

At home, tape yourself on a cassette recorder and play those tapes back. Work for improvement in your speaking technique, and don't stop working. Time spent working from the tapes in your hotel room the night before you speak is time well spent.

Then use a video cassette to study your speaking posture and your technique. If money is no object, hire a media trainer to polish your image and develop those sound bytes.

Step Three: The Early Bird Gets the Book Sales

Arrive early at your speaking site. In advance, ask for a long cloth-covered table set up near the entrance to display books. Check to make sure it's there.

On it, arrange your posters, handout materials, flyers, a few business cards, and your books. Stand one or two upright to catch the audience's attention at the door. Stack plenty of books on the table, or they'll think you have only a few to sell. Better to carry unsold books home, than to miss a sale.

You have a travel bag, right? These are items you'll find indispensable:
- One or two hand-held calculators
- A bag from your local bank to hold checks and money
- A supply of one-dollar bills
- Five or six of your favorite pens for book signing
- A credit-card machine, or Smart card if you have one. Set it up and prominently display it on the table.
- Have a pad of paper or small pieces of paper available.
- Have people print the name they want and hand it to you with the book open to the signature page, or stick the piece on the autograph page.
- On the table near the book stacks, arrange legible small

signs with the price of your book or books and how the buyers are to make out checks

- Display the price(s) on the poster

Ask the event coordinator to have a person available at the table to help with the book signing and collect payments. He or she will open your book to the page to be signed and pass it to you. This expedites the line and gives you a more professional appearance.

Check out the equipment in advance. Microphones vary and so do the height of speakers. Be sure the microphone is positioned for you and look carefully at its location. If the person who introduces you changes the position of the microphone, move it to the correct spot before you begin speaking. Also, be sure the volume is adjusted to a position where you can be heard across the room. Be sure there are no squeals, hums, or other noises to distract the audience from the presentation.

> **HINT:** I like to use a lavaliere microphone when possible. It allows me to roam, covering the stage, gesturing and walking close to the audience. This makes each person feel part of my story.

Avoid alcohol the night before the event, get plenty of sleep, and practice deep breathing. Be sure to have an adequate breakfast with some protein. You don't want to pass out at the podium.

Eat sparingly of the luncheon or dinner menu, and avoid

eating anything too rich or spicy. If you're the least bit nervous, these foods tend to accelerate nerves. Ask the waitperson to leave your dessert for you, and eat it after the book signing.

Prepare your introduction in advance, and mail it to the presenter. When you arrive at the site, go over it with them so there are no mistakes. Have an extra copy of your introduction with you, in case he or she left it at home by the microwave.

Make the introduction short and sweet. Now is the time for your sound byte. Focus on the reason you're there. No one cares how many advanced degrees you have or if you are a great friend to pets. However, if you've recently won a major award for writing, be sure to mention it.

Leave the folder or envelope of note cards at the podium before you speak. Then it's ready to open when you arrive at the podium.

When the audience arrives, mingle with everyone you can. Greet these prospective buyers, and introduce yourself. Make one or two comments about the books and encourage them to look before your presentation. People like to ask informal questions during this time. Be prepared to answer them.

Sometimes you can stand copies of the book or books on the tables near the centerpiece. Encourage the audience to look through the books while the wait-persons are serving.

This isn't possible with a large group, but it focuses a small group's attention on what you're there to talk about. Nine times out of ten, someone at the table will buy the book.

HINT: Depending on the size of the group, offer a first edition copy of the book as a door prize. That generates funds for the organization hosting the program and gets the novel in a new reader's hands.

If I'm invited to a private home, I wrap a book in black silk ribbon and take it as a hostess gift. Either way, post that book in the record log as a gift, not a sale. No sales tax to collect or pay.

Step Four: "Speak the Speech, I Pray You."

Now is the time when all your practice pays off. The presenter has introduced you, and the applause is loud and long. You walk to the podium with confidence. Smile at your audience.

Don't let your terror show, even if your knees are shaking. Stand tall at the dais, position your feet comfortably, legs slightly apart.

Do not grip the podium for dear life. It's not going anywhere. However, if the dais gives you stability, rest your hands lightly on it.

Don't rustle papers nor pick up any nervous habits like removing and replacing your glasses or tapping a pen. Noises carry.

Take a deep breath and begin. Thank the presenter for his or her kind words. You might briefly acknowledge the audience for inviting you with a personalized thank you. "It's great to be here in Miami again and speak to you about my favorite topic." (Be sure you are in Miami and not Midland.)

"It's wonderful to be here to speak to Sisters-in-Crime, a great organization and tremendous supporter of my work."

Begin your speech with a riveting topic sentence designed to draw your audience into your book, why you wrote it, and the way you wrote it.

HINT: A sound byte from your former profession is an excellent way to introduce the speech. One of mine is, "I saw my first dead body when I was twenty-one-years-old." That always gets an audience's attention and makes them want to know more about me and my book.

If you're speaking to a group of writers or pre-published authors, a quote from Ray Bradbury helps break the ice and speaks to reality. "I wrote a million words before I wrote one good one."

If you flub a line, and we all do, do not apologize or get flustered. Keep going. You may have a chance later in your speech to slip in a correction. But make it short, and don't draw attention to it. A good sense of humor will carry you through any difficulty in this area.

HINT: At a California book club luncheon, a female presenter rose to introduce Los Angeles Chief of Police Daryl Gates, who was speaking on his new autobiography, *Chief.*

In her enthusiasm, she said, "It's my pleasure to introduce the biggest cock in the Los Angeles Police Department, Chief Daryl Gates."

The audience roared, but the presenter had no idea what she had said. Chief Gates walked up to the microphone, smiled, and graciously replied, "Yes, I am, thank you."

And the audience laughed louder.

Recite facts and examples, anecdotes, and stories that relate to the book and your experiences.

Don't be afraid to use humor. Be sure, however, the humor is appropriate to the topic and the group. What's funny to the Rodeo Club might seem inappropriate to the Methodist women in your community. Pause after you've said something funny. Enjoy it with the audience. Don't rush your presentation.

Eye contact is most important. You may choose two or three people sitting in different areas of the room and direct your comments to them. Let your eyes sweep from one to the other. Cover the entire room. Or, if looking into the eyes of the audience terrifies you, look slightly over their heads. Don't, however, stare at the ceiling. Your script isn't rolling on cue cards up there.

Focus on the audience. As you become a more practiced speaker, you will learn how to draw the audience to you. Personal touches, even a joke on yourself, make the audience anxious to read your book.

Study other speakers and adapt techniques from them that suit your speaking style. Notice timing, rhythm, and pauses. Appreciate eye contact and facial expressions.

Use appropriate gestures that keep the audience focused on you. Often moving a hand from your body toward the audience shows compassion. Gesturing with an outstretched hand brought into the body brings the audience to you. Don't overdo gestures. Waving your arms like a windmill detracts from good speaking techniques.

Be animated, passionate, and enthusiastic about your speech. Love your audience. As you become a practiced speaker, learn to like these people. After all, they must be nice folks—they came to hear what you have to say. Learn to appreciate each group and what they have to offer.

If this is a large group, ask a monitor to stand or give you a hand motion when you have five minutes left. You have practiced the timing beforehand, of course, but this will give you more security. The more often you present this program, the more proficient you will become.

End your speech on an upbeat note. This doesn't mean saying, "Hey, murder's great. Read all about it." Use an ending that focuses on the great characters in your novel, the practical aspects of your "how-to" book, or what you can learn from the events in your book on local history.

If your program lends itself to questions and answers later, apportion that time, giving forthright and honest answers. People like a back-and-forth discussion with an author. But, don't let one person monopolize your time. Make sure you can conclude your presentation, answer everyone's questions, and allow yourself plenty of time to sign books.

Step Five: Savor the Applause; Sell Those Books

The best speakers will sell themselves, not the book. The audience came to hear you. Through your presentation, they'll learn more about you and like you. The book will sell itself.

If a meeting is to follow your presentation, quietly slip from the head table and sit or stand at the book-signing table, right behind your books, a smile on your face.

If a crowd has gathered at the book-signing area, a gentle nudge at the conclusion of your presentation may stimulate book sales. "Come on over to the signing table so we can talk more."

Make book-signing a personal statement. As you hand the book to the buyer, thank her or him and tell each you hope they enjoy it. "I hope you enjoy reading my book as much as I enjoyed writing it," is one way of saying thanks. A gracious thank you always garners repeat sales and fond memories of you as a speaker.

HINT: I pre-autograph a few of my books—in black ink—at home, long before the event, for buyers who don't want a book personalized or who want to grab a book and run. This guarantees that you never miss a sale. For those wanting the book dedicated all you add is the date and the dedication. This allows time to talk with each customer and make that a personal moment between you and your new fan. You never know who might prove to be the contact person for your next speaking engagement.

Well, you did it. You made it through a speech and a book signing. Your face hurts from smiling, your feet ache, and your throat is dry and raspy. But, you made it. And what a success. No one stood up and booed. No one rushed from the room to avoid your works, and you've autographed a zillion books.

And that's the first zillion. Book signings often result in

repeat sales and new contacts. After all, the word is out—you're a terrific speaker.

Now it's time to repair the damage. Hauling books around takes a lot out of you. Your throat is a precious instrument that helps you sell books, and you must rest and rejuvenate it. Not to mention those aching feet.

If you're on an extended book tour, it's even more important that you preserve your voice. When you travel, always ask your hotel or motel for a quiet, smoke-free room. Now is your time to unwind.

Take off your clothes and those wretched shoes. Retire to your yoga mat or use the pool and exercise equipment.

Treat yourself to room service. You deserve it. Order some hot tea with honey or a light supper. Use your throat spray or simply gargle with warm salt water. Relax, savor your moment—and get ready for the next speaking engagement.

HINT: When you're on the road, even for a short overnight stay, take a goodie bag. Keep plastic bags packed with herb tea, small jars of honey, small plastic salt shakers, throat lozenges, and a bottle of throat spray.

Tuck in quick-energy snacks, such as raisins or dried cranberries. Ginseng and St. John's Wort always travel with me, as does Airborne if I'm traveling by plane. Speaking takes it out of you. Rejuvenation is as close as your pharmacy or health-food store.

With a bubble bath, a good foot rub with peppermint foot cream, and a restful night's sleep, I'm good as new the next day and raring to speak and sell those books.

I always carry night eye shades and ear plugs. And I never leave home without my cervical pillow. We don't need a sleepless night and a headache to mar the next day's presentation.

In addition to my daily vitamins and minerals, I pack emergency supplies of aspirin, nose drops, allergy pills, Band-Aids, eye drops, and cold medication. At the slightest hint of a throat infection brought on by the dust mites in air conditioning filters on airplanes and in airless hotel rooms, I take medication that the doctor prescribes.

And I always carry small bottles of water. I drink lots of water. It reduces the swelling in your limbs and helps the voice. There's nothing so dehydrating as the recycled air in planes, hotels, and conference rooms.

For the next several years—and the next several books—you're going to be speaking, speaking, speaking. To all kinds of groups in all sorts of places. Sometimes the experience won't be enjoyable—in fact, you may prepare for hours, speak to a full house, and not sell a single book. You'll face hecklers. Your hair spray will fail and so will your deodorant. You'll find runs in your hose, or worse, you packed one black shoe and one blue shoe. Life happens.

From now until the day you stop writing, however, it will be part of your life. Learn to enjoy it. Continue to improve your speaking techniques.

Learn which of your anecdotes or stories your audiences appreciate the most. Work to create suspense and interest about your book and your writing.

Soon you're a world-class speaker.

Step 6: What Makes a Speech Successful?

A successful speech has several parts:

- It begins as a concept, an idea, a central thesis. Who is your audience? Why are you there? What is your dowry to the program?
- Add structure, weaving and building on the core. Like telling a story that's revealed a page at a time.
- Create a sound byte that will be remembered long after you've left the podium. Who can forget, "Give me liberty, or give me death?" Or "Ask not what your country can do for you." Or "I have a dream." At Gettysburg, November 19, 1863, Abraham Lincoln spoke for less than three minutes; Edward Everett's speech lasted two hours. Which speech do you remember?
- Weave the presentation until the cloth is complete.
- End with a bang and make them beg for more.
- Tell them you're going to tell them something. Tell them. Then tell them you told them.

No matter how experienced you are at public speaking, always outline the presentation. Then tighten, trim words, rehearse, and tighten it again. Listen to yourself, and you'll hear what works and what doesn't. Practice for the family, the mirror, or close friends. Listen to constructive criticism. You're doing this for several reasons:

- To hear the weak spots
- To memorize bits and pieces
- To test the time-line. There's nothing as boring as a thirty-minute speaker dragging on for almost an hour.

Transitions and humor are excellent changes to test audience attention. Don't be cute, unless you can carry it off. There's only one Jay Leno.

Symbols, metaphors, and quotations bring the audience on the ride you're taking. The key is customizing those to your speech. If they're Democrats, don't quote a Republican. Don't quote William Buckley, when it should be Gore Vidal. Know your audience.

Several recommended speech sources are:

- *Bartlett's Famous Quotations* by John Bartlett
- *Secrets of Successful Speakers* by Lilly Walters
- *The Greatest Speakers I Ever Heard* by Dottie Walters

Don't miss *How to Build Your Speaking and Writing Empire* presented by Mark Hanson and Jack Canfield, our *Chicken Soup* friends. It's the most powerful weekend you'll ever invest in. To book Mark contact ChrisLee@calendar.com 877-1855 x 101, Mark Victor Hansen, P. O. Box 7665, Newport Beach, CA 92658-7665; (949) 524-1500. http://www.markvictorhansen.com http://www.chickensoup.com

If your budget includes media training dollars, remember the more exposure you have, the more books fly off the shelves. Highly trained image professionals cost big bucks, so unless you want to tape an infomercial, you're better off having family members tape you or stand in front of a mirror and practice.

You can buy an excellent video entitled *You're on the Air* from Book Marketing Works.com. P.O. Box 715, Avon, CT 06001-0715. (860) 675-1344. If you're serious about media training, kits, and much more, Brian Jud bjud@bookmarketing.com

National Seminars Group/Padgett-Thompson, a division of Rockhurst University Continuing Education Center,

Inc. at P.O. Box 419107 Kansas City, MO 64141-6107, offers interactive CDs *How to Write Copy that Sells* and *Microsoft PowerPoint Supercharged with Multimedia.* (800) 258-7246, (913) 432-7755. http://www.nationalseminarstraining.com

Speak and Get Paid for It. Dottie Walters was founding President and CEO of one of the world-renowned speaker bureaus, Walters International Speakers Bureau. She taught me and many others how to help you find those paying customers. Send a one page, how-to article to *Sharing Ideas,* her magazine for entrepreneurial speakers. You are automatically represented by her firm when they print your article. P. O. Box 398, Glendora, CA 91740. (626) 335-8069. speakandgrowrich.com http://www.walters-intl.com info@walters-intl.com Check out the video on YouTube: https://www.youtube.com/watch?v=GuBM4FIH1dY

Maybe your forte is as a lecturer, trainer, educator. *Fred Pryor Seminars/Career Track* trains more than 750,000 people each year throughout the world. It offers seminars on every topic imaginable. Being an author is a plus. If you're interested in employment opportunities, Email Human Resources Department at careeropportunities@pryor.com, or FAX your resume with cover letter and salary history to (913) 967-8581. Then submit a training video shot of you in front of a live audience, a resume or press kit, and a list of topics you're an expert on. Contact the Trainer Recruiter, 9757 Metcalf Avenue, Overland Park, KS 66212. (800) 780-8476, customerservice@pryor.com or http://www.pryor.com

That wasn't so hard. Now let's get all your tools together in Chapter Three.

CHAPTER 3

It's Tool Time

If you're talking with another author and writing your name and address on scraps of paper as your business introduction, let's introduce you to a number of products that will bring you into the 21st century. Below is an inventory of writing tools the ideal office should have. Cost factors may place some items on your wish list for a later date. The key is to prioritize what you must have now to be professional, and what you can farm out, like printing and copying services.

Business Cards

Don't scrimp on budget dollars when it comes to stationery and business cards. Scraps of paper, the back of a deposit slip, or worse yet, the back of someone else's business card is not the professional way to network. It isn't advisable to pour out the contents of a purse or take everything out of the wallet that has been smashed in your rear pocket in search of a card. Keep them in a small briefcase, the conference tote, or a cardholder—fresh, crisp, not bent or dingy.

Software makes creating business cards, brochures, and letterheads a snap. Paper Direct is one source. Call

(800) 272-7377, for their free catalog.

And don't print too many at a time. Zip codes change. So do area codes. Don't cross out old numbers. Opt instead to make fresh, new cards and stationery.

Never leave home without them. They're especially important at book signings, conventions, conferences, and seminars. Exchange them with the world.

When you give one away, get one in return. Those cards are the building blocks of potential fans and/or clients. Networking builds mailing lists. That person may also have special training that will assist you in writing. Every card is a source for some marketing portion of your career.

Send a card out in all first-time correspondence, including paying bills. Leave one on restaurant dining tables with your tip, and put one in the counter jars for free lunch drawings. Get to know your locals. You need name recognition.

Should they be fancy or plain? Colored card stock or iridescent material? Professional? Or computer generated?

Harlan Ellison's card states simply, "I write."

Raul Melendez has the name of his debut novel, *Mercy Street,* on the front of his card and a brief synopsis of the story on the back.

Lawrence Block's card bears no mention that he's a prolific mystery author, teacher, and mentor. Only his name, address, phone and fax number, in black ink, appears on a pure white card.

Thom Racina has a black linen card with white ink, giving us addresses in both Palm Springs, California, and Washington, D.C.

ATTORNEY AT LAW Joseph Fleischmann, II has a marbleized pink and cream-colored card.

Marcia Talley puts her book jacket photo on the left side of the card. The title, *Sing it to Her Bones* is at the top, followed by the name of her series. The balance of her card contains her contact information.

The point here is to be creative. You are the writer. Your business card is an extension of you.

Private Box Number

There are a lot of strange people out there. Not your fans, of course, but others. Insulate yourself, and protect your home privacy with a postal box. You can rent from the post office or one of the many commercial postal services located in neighborhood shopping centers near you.

The post office box is inexpensive at about $200 a year. Commercial company prices vary from $40 to $300 annually. If you use a postal service, select a private one that doesn't charge premiums for postage or packaging. Many do. And don't rent the largest box. Both places will leave you a "you have a big item" slip when your box fills with royalty checks. Best of all, the rental expense is tax deductible against your earnings.

And while you're on tour, both will collect your mail so it doesn't pile up at home.

Telephone

Answer professionally, even if it is your home phone. On the answering machine, leave a warm, creative message. And update often. Don't talk about the snowfall when it's summertime. Abruptness or some old cliché, "This is an answering machine, you know what to do," will get you the desired result. They will hang up. This is a marketing tool. Develop a positive message. Draw the caller into your realm. Want them to beg to speak with you, after all, they found your special and probably unlisted telephone number. And you're going to be a famous author.

Whenever possible, answer the telephone yourself. Don't ask anyone to "Pound One" to leave a message for you.

In *The Excellence Challenge*, author Tom Peters wrote, "The only magic of the $40 billion giant IBM is that in a $500 billion industry they happen to be the only company that still answers the phone."

1-800 or 1-888 Numbers

If the direct mail concept works for your product, these toll-free services that connect you to your customer base are a must. To achieve the best return for this expense, you must accept credit cards, and should have a 24-hour day, 7-day week answering service. To check on current rates, call:

- AT&T Customer Service (800) 225-5288
- MCI Telecommunications (800) 444-3333
- Sprint Dial "1" Service (877) 4020
- Verizon (800) 837-4966

For those of you who don't expect a high volume of calls, maybe a toll-free answering service fits your criteria. A current list can be found in *The Complete Direct Marketing Sourcebook*.

Press Kits and Photos

The press kit is the most important tool you have as a writer. As you develop into a professional writer, lecturer, and teacher, this tool will undergo many changes. Allow for flexibility. You'll need photographs and several enclosures. Let's start with the pictures.

Color or black and white? As former Dallas Cowboy, Deion Sanders often says, "Both."

This is another area you cannot skimp on the budget funds. Contact local photographers and get bids. The photographer for your newspaper may be an independent contractor who knows exactly what you need and when you need it. Pay a deposit only, not the entire session fee, until you get an opportunity to view and approve the photos and negatives.

Negotiate for the proofs and/or the opportunity to print in greater quantity later. You own the negatives. When you need to reorder, take them to a less expensive developer for reprints. The black-and-white glossy photo is a must for newsletters and newspapers. It's the real person you are, the one that will appeal to the media.

Don't try tricky poses or place your hands or other objects next to your face. The newspapers often "crop" pictures to fit the width of the columns and the length of the space. When cut to size, the hand may look as if it belongs to someone who isn't in the picture.

If you wear glasses, find a pair of empty frames similar to the ones you usually wear. This reduces glare. The camera needs to photograph your eyes, not the lens.

Ask the photographer for 5 x 7's or 3 x 4's. They are cheaper to develop and easier to let go of. The newspaper will not normally return the photograph. If you're local, they should have a "morgue," or library of photos, and will save yours for future use. If you must have the photo back, include a SASE with a request.

There are some photographers talented enough to make you younger, thinner, or less wrinkled. But, miracles only happen in the movies. At least, you should expect a clear, good portrait that is flexible enough to meet all your needs.

After you've gone to all this trouble, don't get your feelings hurt if the article is published without your photo. It's a matter of time and space. Nothing personal.

> **HINT:** For my first book a very long time ago, I went to a glamour shot store at the local mall with my gun (after getting permission from the mall owner, of course) and did a major "big hair and lots of sexy makeup" color shot for both my press kit and the book jacket. Total cost $75.
>
> The black-and-white in a more formal studio ran $250, but I own the proofs and the opportunity to print more copies at a future date for a reduced price.
>
> Regarding the book jacket, be imaginative here. If your book is about animals, take the shot with your animal or better yet, photograph the animal alone. You can create mystique by not showing your photo at all on the jacket. The strength of a photo can turn them on or off. It will generate interest to get you read or negatively tossed in the trash can. It's that important.

> For your first book, link your photo to the theme or book topic. You're defining not only your creative style throughout the tour, but your life as a writer as well.

Press Kits

Buy bright, flat, not glossy 9" x 12" pocket folders from the local office supply store. Jewel-toned red, blue, and green are particularly popular colors. Put your card in the slot on the left-hand side and your photo in the pocket behind that; enclose any value-added marketing item you've developed.

> **HINT:** I slip one of my book markers and a postcard that has my book jacket cover on it in front of the photo.

On the right-hand side place, the following in order:
- A fact sheet that has the title, author name, publisher, number of pages, ISBN number, publication date, binding and price in both the United States and Canada
- A synopsis (or excerpts) of the book, one or two pages in length
- A one-page author bio
- Press releases tied to current "hot" news
- Newspaper clippings
- Book quotes from reviewers and/or other readers
- An itinerary, if the tour has been partially scheduled, to enhance the value of your presentation

- A prepared list of twenty questions that an interviewer from television, radio or magazine might ask. Provide the answers, too. Make them direct, funny, sharp, and crisp. This will help the host, who may not already know you and will jumpstart your interview. If they haven't read the book yet, it will help them seem more informed and less embarrassed.

When you first build this kit, you'll have very little in the way of press releases, clips, or quotes. You may start with a "thank you" letter from a book signing event, and/or a quote from someone in the genre who loved the book. Quotes and testimonials from amateurs will also work for the first time kit. Use large fonts to make those few fill an entire page for volume.

These items will be discarded later in favor of professional reviews from *Publishers Weekly, Kirkus Review,* and *Library Journal.* And from fans who'll email you and/or place their review of the book on Amazon.com or Barnes & Noble.com.

A complete list of quotes is an important part of the press kit. Type them on one sheet, with the most powerful and visible one at the top.

You may wish to include published articles that relate to your product. This reinforces that you are the expert on this topic.

Some authors include a copy of the book jacket. You should ask the publisher for the overprints anyway. A hundred or so is not an unreasonable request. If it's a hardback, carry extras to the bookstores and replace those that have been damaged.

These kits must also be modular in form. Allow the flexibility to reach specific audiences. If you want to be a speaker or on a panel, focus on your speaking credits. If your repertoire includes other venues, like your career, a sheet profiling your expertise will achieve the best result.

Letterheads and Envelopes for your Stationery

Your manuscript is done in Courier or Times New Roman type, 12 point, on white bond paper. That is a professional style that works well for your stationery as well.

Other variations define you as an amateur. And, even if you are, don't tell anyone. Envelopes are #10 size. As in your selection of material for your business cards, the paper defines you. If you're the iridescent pink and silver type with butterflies, go for it.

Zip Code Book and Postal Scale

With the mobility of our population, regional changes throughout the United States occur often. Twenty to thirty percent of the addresses on your mailing list will change every year. A zip code book is critical in the care and maintenance of your mailing list, not to mention that accuracy expedites your correspondence.

The postal scale is an inexpensive purchase. When you conduct a mass mailing, concentrate on the size and weight of the items to be mailed for cost efficiency. There's nothing more embarrassing than to send out correspondence and not have sufficient postage. If you're a "do it yourself" person, try Stamps.com from 12959 Coral Tree Place, Los Angeles, CA 90066-7020. They'll provide you with a digital scale and ability to print your own postage in one inexpensive package.

Bulk Mail

If you have less than 200 pieces for Standard Mail, or 500 pieces for First Class to be mailed at the same time, bulk mail may be the less expensive way.

The keys to saving money are:

- Getting the mail, the right size and shape for the post office to process it.
- Printing your addresses so they can be scanned by an optical character reader or barcode sorter.
- Presorting the mail by Zip Code.
- Grouping the mail into packages in certain numbers.
- Placing the packages into trays or sacks provided by the post office.
- Delivering it to the post office. They don't offer home or office pick-up for bulk mail.

While your mailing list will be cleaned periodically, having the new codes expedite this tedious work. Software from sources like *MyMailList* is a writer's boon. You can get this product through Avanquest Publishing USA, Pleasanton, CA 94566. (877) 445-6618 http//www.avanquestusacom for a free catalog. http://www.avanquestusa.com. *MyMailList Deluxe* software offers complete mail list management, mail design, printing, and bulk mail solutions. You may need to ask for a permit application. There's an annual fee of $29.95.

To learn more about bulk mail; http://www.usps.gov

Postal Explorer is a virtual library of postal information designed for business mailers. PE contains several documents including the Domestic Mail Manual (DMM) and the International Mail Manual (IMM). http://www.pe.usps. com/cpim/ftp/manuals/dmm300/full/MailingStandards.pdf You can order a printed copy of the DMM or IMM online at http://pe.usps.com/cpim/ftp/manuals/imm/full/imm.pdf.

Of course, if you develop a database on the computer, individual emails also keep you in touch with your audience. And don't forget you have your own EXCEL spreadsheet if you want to keep track of addresses.

Shipping Boxes and Large Envelopes

The mark of a well-informed, seasoned author who ships thick manuscripts will include the use of boxes:

- Don't forget all your office supply houses near you. If you're buying in bulk, it's Papermart.com
- Papyrus Papers 300 Oak Bluff Lane, Goodettesville, TN 37072 (800) 789-1649 info@papyrusplace.com or http://www.papyrusonline.com

When shipping your manuscript, place stamps on the inside box with your return address on that box. The outside box can be canceled with a postal meter, but stamps are a must on the inside one.

If you prefer envelopes to boxes, compare postal rates. Depending on the number of pages being mailed, the postage for the box is often less expensive. Book rates for boxes simply cost less money.

Calendars

Make a calendar for you, the publicist, your agent, and your family. They should all conform with dates, including family blackout times for vacation and life. You do have a life, you know. Enter everything in pencil. You will have to change dates, and make sure every person is notified of those changes to avoid double booking.

Computer and Printer

Buy what you can afford to have and maintain it. The computer software capability is as important or more important than the computer and should drive what you buy. Whether you invest in a major name brand product, by mail order through a computer warehouse, or inherit a used computer and printer, strive for top computer speed and memory.

> **HINT**: Because of the number of projects I'm working on at any given time, I have installed Dragon Systems' Naturally Speaking and dictate much of my work. Dan Poynter in his *Write and Grow Rich* book explains this program best. I miss you, Dan.

Use a high-resolution laser printer. No professional writer uses dot matrix anymore. The manuscript paper is clear, white, bond. Fancy papers or colors clearly define you as an amateur, not as a maverick. To advance your writing career, this is an areawhere you want to quietly fit in.

Fax Machine and Scanner

75% of all business-to-business transactions will be via the fax or scanner. When you need to proof documents, send out part of your press kit to a prospective client, or speak with someone in another time zone and who's difficult to reach, its speed makes this piece of office equipment a must.

If the fax or scanner is built into your personal computer, all the better. It saves both time and paper.

The Official Facsimile Users' Directory lists over 30,000 Fax numbers. The *Fax Phone Book* has almost 200,000 additional numbers. Add your name to those directories.

Others include Bowker's *Book Trade Fax & Phone Directory* in paperback

Label Maker

No author can live without a label maker. It saves hours no writer can afford to waste. Make sure your software has the capacity to sort in zip code order.

- NEBS, Inc. offers the maker and software. (888) 823-6327 customerservice@nebs.com or order online at http://www.nebs.com and deluxe.com/shop
- Seiko Instruments offers several makers and the software to manage it. Contact them at 1130

I use Smart Label printer for small jobs. Seiko SII and their labels are available at all office supply houses and online orders.

> **HINT**: I started a mailing list with family, close friends, and clients from my former working life. Everyplace I go, I exchange cards with fans, writers, promoters, bookstore owners, people in line at the bank, the grocery, and the airport—everywhere. That inner circle of names, now in excess of 15,000, has become the most important part of my promotional dowry. These people get advance notice if I'm speaking in their area when a new book comes out, or if I'm going to be on television or radio in their city.

Don't forget these people at Christmas. It's not only a way of thanking them for being a part of your life, but it washes the list for address accuracy.

Join writing groups. They have mailing lists. Obtain a list of key media contacts, both locally and through the *Literary Market Place*. Join social, volunteer, church, and/or fraternal organizations. See how the names and address list multiplies beyond your inner circle.

Buy association mailing lists that cover a broad range of topics including medical and engineering. MGILists at 625 W. Washington Street, Alexandria, VA 22314-1930. (800) 899-4420, (703) 739-1000, mgilists@mgilists.com or http://www.mgilists.com

Goodies, T-shirts, Mugs, Tote Bags…Swag

T-shirts are walking billboards: expressive and individual. They're inexpensive marketing tools for raffles, gift baskets, presents, and conferences.

Try CompressedTShirt.com, a division of the Idea Express Promotional Group. Their T-shirts are folded into postcard shapes, ready for mailing. They have online quotes. (858) 558-8500 compressedtshirts.com

For more creative ideas for marketing, look at CafePress. com a site with more than 4 million members.

> **HINT**: During a slow book signing night at a Texas mall, I found a kiosk that silk-screened T-shirts, gave them a copy of my book and had T-shirts made up for several fans. Very inexpensive and clever.

For postcards, business cards, address labels, or bookmarks, check for local printers. Sometimes the expense and time factor are important. For others compare prices by shopping with organizations like Premier Promotions, JerryJones@ premierpromos.com

Mugs and tote bags can also be silk-screened. These items are expensive because they must be purchased in volume. There usually isn't a decent price break until an order reaches 5,000 items.

As an alternative, use the camera-ready artwork from your zip disk and save a lot of money. Better yet, drop by the local arts and crafts store and buy the totes. They come in several colors and fabrics. Create your own with stencils, patterns or other materials.

Try buttons, caps, magnets, key-chains, or T-shirts that say, "Ask me about my ISBN number." Or "Have you read my book?" will catch some eyes. How about, "I'm a writer. For me, this is dressed up." These make wonderful point-of-purchase items at the bookstore cash register and/or stuffer gifts for the convention tote bags.

Bumper stickers and license plate frames are great visuals when you're on the road. The swap meet near your home will customize them with your message quite inexpensively.

> **HINT:** I did bookmarks that looked like police caution tape. Thirty-five hundred should cost less than $300. I chose bright yellow with black letters. On one side it read: CAUTION: POLICE LINE—DO NOT CROSS. On the other, in addition to the book title was the ISBN number, the publisher's name, and the website address. I had them UV coated so they'd be sturdy and last longer. People loved them. I gave those away to strangers everywhere I traveled.

Flyers and Brochures

Computer software has made this important tool incredibly easy to modify and maintain. Create them for press kits and individual mailings. They are a must for the speaker bureaus that will hire you. Use four-color, glossy paper on the front side with your photo and several bullets about your presentation.

Use black and white on the back side listing all the organizations and places you've spoken.

These can be done on a home computer using a software program. Each presentation will have a different topic. And as your experiences grow, so does the list of your clients. Flexibility is the key to keeping this important tool current.

Access to a Central Library

A great deal of information for the writer is available in the library, including the oft times referred to: *Literary Market Place (LMP)*. Libraries can't afford current year editions, but the *LMP* is now online. When you are looking for a source, you will be contacting the resource direct to verify they're still in business, the address is correct, and the editor is the person who will review your project.

Credit Cards

If direct mail is a good source for selling your product, apply to all major credit cards. Apply for PayPal off your website. Not every customer will want to use cash, checks, or money orders. This country runs on credit. Contact your bank and ask for VISA and MasterCard application forms. You are "seeking credit card merchant status."

For others:

American Express

Discover Card/Visa/MasterCard

Website

In this electronic age, the importance of the internet and the role it plays in your success has a chapter all its own. (See Chapter Nine.) But as a tool, you should know that a website is an extension of your press kit. Check out other writer's and publisher's websites. What do you like? What doesn't work for you? How can your site represent your product in its highest form? This is a very inexpensive advertising item that keeps you and your fans in touch.

> **HINT**: Mine, http://www.joycespizerfoy.com, contains a current personal message, a photo gallery, and book jacket covers, my appearance schedule, quotes from fans, links to other sites, contact info, and most important of all, Pay Pal for ordering books. Talk about shameless promotion.

Email

Email is the ultimate tool for the millennium. Every 24 hours, more than 70 million people in America use email. It keeps your fans in touch, yet maintains your privacy. This address goes on the business card, the letterhead, and in the press kit. List it in organizational directories and on your website. Now it's time to get organized.

CHAPTER 4

Get Organized

This chapter is not about organizing your work. Book selling is a marketing war. Marketing is about finding, nurturing, and maintaining relationships. People want value. Offer them more than they expect. Join organizations. Lots of them.

Why? Because writing is a solitary, insular business. Organizational memberships provide a variety of benefits.

Writing organizations create networks, have conferences, print newsletters, sell advertising, have wonderful mailing lists, chat groups, and offer opportunities to spotlight your talent. Genre groups like Romance Writers of America and Sisters-in-Crime are outstanding examples of those that showcase members.

Education, information, and up-to-date pulse readings on America's ever-changing publishing industry are major pluses to membership.

Join the king. Publishers Marketing Association where networking and learning are keys to your success. info@IBPA-online.org and https://www.ibpa-online.org. It's also International Book Publishing Association or IBPA and is an online education and networking group located at Box 1020, Manhattan Beach, CA 90266 (310) 546-1818.

Another group is SPAN, the Small Publishers

Association of North America. span@spannet.org and http://www. spannet.org

> **HINT:** I once belonged to eighteen organizations; fourteen of them were professional writing groups when my first book was published. Why would I involve myself in so many when I need to write? How did I select the organizations? How did they help my project? Read on.

If marketing is war, then put on your armor. Join organizations. Why? Consider the following reasons:

They offer a strong sense of satisfaction and define you as the person you are. Networking and bonding with other writers offer encouragement. You'll receive expert assistance from professionals, find educational resources, and up-to-date information in your field. Many offer health insurance, educational benefits, appearances at conferences, book festival, etc.

If you're self-published, joining increases purchasing clout and exposure to those you wouldn't otherwise meet. Learn from them.

A few organizations provide reasonably priced medical and dental benefits. There may be opportunities for freelance work that also brings you recognition.

Some groups offer critique services. Others will advise you regarding literary agencies and agents. While others may provide mentoring programs. Local chapters maintain audio and video tape libraries of speakers and many hold competitions, offer awards, have monthly local meetings, and annual national conventions.

The Writers' League of Texas is an all-genre full-service organization. They help writers promote and sell their work. They provide resources, publications, educational opportunities, media exposure, special events, and networking.

The National Writer's Association is another all-genre organization. They are located at 10940 S. Parker Road, #508, Parker, CO 80134. Contact them at (303) 841-0246 http://www.nationalwriters.com natlwritersassn@hotmail.com Chapters meet monthly throughout the United States. Networking, information, and addressing the needs of the local writers are their main objectives. NWA offers critique services, freelance opportunities in their *Authorship Magazine,* agent recommendations, contests, award programs, and conventions. Their online service promotes the author's product, including links to websites.

Romance Writers of America is located at 14615 Benfer Road, Houston, Texas 77069 (832) 717-5200. They have 10,000 members in 35 countries. info@rwa.org or https://www.rwa.org Don't think of Danielle Steele and romance. This genre includes exotic alternatives to the "bosom rippers" you've heard about. Think: mystery, cozy, historical, western, intrigue, inspirational, contemporary, mainstream, time travel, new age, and paranormal.

Sisters-in-Crime's world headquarters can be contacted at P. O. Box 442124, Lawrence, KS 66044; (758) 842-1325. admin@sistersincrime.org or http://www.sistersincrime.org. This international group of "sisters" includes many "brothers." If you're a mystery fan, pre-published or published author, this is the organization for you.

Founded in 1897, National League of American Pen

Women greets artists, composers, and writers. 1300 17th NW, Washington, D.C. 20036 (202) 785-1997 NLAPW.org

Western Writers was founded in 1953 for artists, writers, songwriters, poets and storytellers. Westernwriters.org

Mystery Writers of America organized in 1945 is a prestigious writing organization and presents the EDGAR award annually. 1140 Broadway #1507, New York, New York 10001 (212) 888-8171 https://mysterywriters.org.

Science Fiction Writers of America (founded in 1965) offers an annual Nebula award and has 1900 sci-fi and fantasy members. Box 3238, Enfield, CT 06083-3238 sfwa.org

Organizations you select should have:

- Magazines and newsletters that offer "how-to" articles
- Freelance opportunities
- Editing and critique services
- Monthly local meetings where you network with other writers, meet professional instructors and experts in all fields
- Kudo pages where you tout your new novel and the tour
- A mailing list and host an annual and/ or regional conference.
- Local chapters with regular meetings

It's your job not to nitpick, but to network. In networking, you can't imagine how many strange, wonderful, and funny people you will meet. Some will become lifelong friends. Others will remain fellow writers. You may find a publicist, a lawyer, or an accountant who will become a character in one of your future novels.

Or you may fulfill your need to volunteer and help others.

Whatever your reason, join.

Remember the most important tool to selling your novel is finding buyers. Your mailing list is your dowry, what you bring to the publishing table.

> **HINT:** Imagine the raised eyebrows in 1990, when I initially mentioned my mailing list contained over 5,700 names. That number did not include the organizational membership lists. Remember, you only need to sell 25,000 hardback copies of your book to reach the best seller list. Start that mailing list today. Give a card. Get a card.

Many of these organizations offer monthly meetings and have fascinating and educational speakers in the fields of law enforcement, forensics, medical and legal, and other experts. These people become resources for information you may need later in your writing. You'll find many friends in these "like" groups. They also open doors for speaking opportunities if you have a special field of expertise.

> **HINT:** A longtime acquaintance of mine is a former FBI agent. We spoke at several speaking circuits and billed ourselves as the Hunk and the Bag Lady. I'm the one carrying a bag with handout goodies that the FBI allowed as public information to educate the public.

Writing organizations, both national and local, have magazines and newsletters. This media broadens the audience for your freelance work, an announcement regarding your new book, or an ad outlining your scheduled tour.

They may teach you how to negotiate a contract, sell short stories you've written, or write freelance articles.

Attend writing conferences. Local, state, regional, national, and worldwide conferences are all very important extensions of your success. They educate, create visibility for you, and help you develop name recognition. You'll meet new friends, sit on panels, conduct book signings, and meet lots of famous writers.

Speaker Bureaus

Don't forget the speaker bureaus. This is an untapped market resource for many writers. If you have an expertise or specialty career, develop a variety of different programs and pitch yourself on the talk circuit. They pay very well and you sell books.

Join several professional speaker bureaus or create your own. For someone who has written a book and has a repertoire of programs, they can command speaking fees ranging from $750 to $2,000. Whether you live in a resort area, a metropolitan city, or a small community, don't miss a fabulous opportunity to meet people from around the world who attend conferences and conventions. And buy books.

Check the local Yellow Pages and the internet for speaker bureaus in your area. You may not command six-figure fees, but the honorarium pays bills, helps you perfect your author persona and sound bytes, and boosts you into the realm of the "recognized."

Several national bureaus include:

- Walters International Speakers Bureau at P. O. Box 398, Glendora, CA 91740; (626) 335-8069, Refer to a listing and info earlier in the book. Their international magazine, *Sharing Ideas,* offers major exposure to the writer/speaker.
- Speakers Platform at http://www.speaking.com showcases speakers and trainers for the international market. 611 S. Palm Canyon Drive, #7466, Palm Springs, CA 92264 (877) 717-5327 and (760) 656-8770. speaker@speaking.com
- Tu-Vets Corporation for full-color flyers from 1,250 to 20,000 copies. Contact them at 5635 E. Beverly Blvd, Los Angeles, CA 90022; (323) 724-8975. info@tu-vets.com http://www.tu-vets.com
- *Speakers for Free* http://freespeakerbureau.com
- *Association News* (Schneider Publishing Company) is an independent magazine for associations. If your product and knowledge match specific groups or if you're looking for meeting planners, contact them at 11835 West Olympic Boulevard, 12th Floor, Los Angeles, CA 90064. (877) 577-3700. Executive Event Plannerinfo@schneiderpublishing.com http://www.associationnews.com

Remember, you're developing resources to help you write your second novel and promote you and your book.

Along the way, you'll meet experts in fields that may come in handy for a future project. Need an anthropologist? How about a family therapist? Maybe a retired FBI agent? They're out there waiting to help you.

No book signing or speech is too small or unimportant unless distance or expense is an issue.

> **HINT:** I spoke at a local library before twenty people. A young Brit asked a lot of questions, asked for my card and left without buying a book. I sold six books that day. However, that young man emailed me later and offered me an opportunity to speak at a major bookstore. That gig led to seven more book signings. And the book sales eventually exceeded six hundred.

If you're the expert in your field, help others find you with these helpful hints:
- If your product dictates, advertise in card packs.
- Add a page in the very back of the book, offering a discount coupon for the purchase of a future book, or another copy of that book, or a rebate for volume purchasing.
- Request they contact you by email and/or your 1-800 number for speaking engagements.
- Autograph your book and donate them for auctions and raffles. Decorate baskets that include the novel. If your book is a love story add a soft background music tape, candles, and sparkling water.

Library Information

Libraries are organizations too. They have a budget and buy

books, especially from local authors. They also offer reading programs where you can speak and sell to the public.

R.R. Bowker LLC will rent library mailing lists if you specifically request genre information. Corporate offices: 630 Central Avenue, New Providence, NJ 07974; (800) 526-9537, (908) 286-1090, info@bowker.com Customer Service: (888) 269-5372, CustomerService@bowker.com or http://www.bowker.com

Some major reional library systems include:

- Atlanta-Fulton Public Library System, One Margaret Mitchell Square NW, Atlanta, GA 30303-1089, (404) 730-1700 http://AFPLS.org
- Buffalo & Erie County Public Library System, 1 Lafayette Square, Buffalo, New York 14203, (716) 858-8900 http://buffalolib.org
- Harold Washington Library Center, 400 South State Street, Chicago, IL 60605, (312) 747-4999 or 747-4300 http://www.chipublib.org
- Dallas Public Library, 1515 Young Street, Dallas, Texas 75201-5499, (214) 670-1400, (214) 670-1700 http://dallaslibrary2.org/central/index.php
- Denver Public Library, 10 West 14th Avenue Parkway, Denver, CO 80204-2731, (720) 865-1111, (720) 865-1728 denverlibrary.org
- Free Library of Philadelphia, Central Library Logan Square, 1901 Vine Street, Philadelphia, PA 19103. (215) 686-5322, (215) 686-5360 freelibrary.org
- Hawaii State Library, Contact them at 478 South King Street, Honolulu, HI 96813-2901. (808) 586-3500 or (808) 586-3617 http://hawaii.sdp.sirsi.net/client/default
- Houston Public Library, 500 McKinney Avenue,

Houston, TX 77002-2534, (832) 393-1313 <u>Houstonli-</u><u>brary.org</u>
- Los Angeles County <u>colapublib.org</u> <u>skyepatricklibrary-</u><u>director@library.lacounty.gov</u>
- Miami-Dade Public Library System, Main Library, 101 W. Flagler Street, Miami, FL 33130, (305) 375-2665 <u>http://www.mdpls.org</u>
- Multnomah County Library, Central Library, 801 S.W. 10th Avenue, Portland, OR 97205-2520, (503) 988-5123 <u>multcolib.org</u>
- New York Public Library, Science, Industry and Business Library, 476 5th Ave, New York, NY 10018, (212) 592-7000, (212) 930-8000
- Rocky River Public Library, 1600 Hampton Road, Rocky River, OH 44116. (440) 333-7610 <u>rrpl.org</u>
- Salt Lake City Public Library System, 210 East 400 South, Salt Lake City, UT 84111, (801) 524-8200 <u>slcpl.</u><u>org</u>
- San Diego County Library, Central Library, 5500 Over-land Ave, San Diego, CA 92123 (619) 858-694-2415
- San Francisco Public Library, 100 Larkin Street, San Francisco, CA 94102-4733, (415) 557-4400
- Seattle Public Library, 1000 Fourth Avenue, Seattle, WA 98104-1109, (206) 386-4636

Other Mailing Lists

Buy mailing lists and databases like:
- <u>PublicityHound.com</u> <u>jstewart@publicityhound.com</u>,

Box 437, Pt Washington, WI 530-0437 (262) 284-7451

- Lists: <u>nextmark.com</u> is mailing list finder with over 60,000 contacts.
- *Burrelle's Media Directory* at <u>directory@burrelles.com</u> or 800-368-8070 is also a proven resource burrellsluce. com

---

Buying from the Government

And don't forget the largest organization of them all, our "men and women in uniform." This is an untapped resource for sales. At any given time, the United States government has more than one million personnel in the armed forces stationed all over the world. They read books, and they buy from the PX. But, as you might suspect, selling to the government is an art.

Write the Superintendent of Documents, U.S. Government Printing Office, 732 North Capitol Street, Washington, D.C. 20401, (866) 512-1800, (202) 512-1800 gpo.gov

---

Selling to the Prison Systems

Unicor and the FBI have their book buying tied to budgets and that differs in both the state and federal prison systems.

John Kremer, the self-publishing expert has an article about that in Open Horizons, Box 2887 Taos, NM 87571 <u>bookmarket.com/tipprisons</u>

Donating to Charity

For the charitable organizations in your life, designate a charity to receive a portion of your net proceeds. This can be announced on the acknowledgment page of your book, your website, on a separate flyer, a poster, or at a special event for that charity.

Now that you're organized and have the physical and speaking tools – let's move those books.

CHAPTER 5

Who, When, and How
to "Book 'em"

What about the tour? Jacqueline Susann may have been the creator of the celebrity/author tour when she promoted *Valley of the Dolls* in 1966. But for the rest of us, book signing tours began in the 1980's at a time when independent bookstores made up more than 50% of the book selling market. Remember those days before the major chains? The box stores? The coffee and soft comfortable chairs? Before Amazon.com. and Barnes & Noble.com?

Terry McMillan thumped and stumped promoting her first novel, *Mama*. By the time *Waiting to Exhale* was published, the booksellers approached her.

Is the book tour dead? Elaine Petrocelli, with Book Passage in Corte Madera once said, "We have events at 8 a.m. that are so big we have to rent the theater next door."

Algonquin Publishing of Chapel Hill, North Carolina, employed a unique tactic to promote Ann Mariah Cook's *Running North*. Reported in *Publishers Weekly (PW)*, on March 15, 1999, they sent Ms. Cook, an accomplished dog sledder, along with several other dog-sled teams through the snow on book tour between New Hampshire bookstores. They served hot chocolate and pastries and videotaped the event. The sign-ings made national news and, most importantly, they sold all the books in stock in both stores.

Imagine Anne Rice on a three-month bus book tour in 1995, during which time she also wrote a travel diary for an online magazine. She combined her bookstore appearances with blood drives in many cities. After all, she knows vampires.

Those who gave blood were given a button that read, "I gave blood to the Vampire Armand," and they jumped to the head of her book signing table as their reward. If you ever stood in line for Anne's autograph, you know what a great perk that was.

Courageous mystery writers, Martin J. Smith and Philip Reed, piled their kids into a minivan and toured the country together during one, four-week, ten-state summer odyssey. They bravely took this trip without their wives.

In 1992, Sarah Weeks committed to a forty-city tour to launch her debut novel and cassette package, *Crocodile Smith*. She carried a karaoke player, which at the time wasn't as well-known as it is today.

In the "you shoulda' been there" department, Patricia Cornwell, who earned her helicopter pilot's license, bought a 'copter after having a Scarpetta logo emblazoned on its side. On August 7, 1999, she piloted solo and landed in the park-ing lot of a major book chain in her hometown of Richmond, Virginia.

Kevin J. Anderson, author of twenty-five novels includ-ing *Ai! Pedrito!*, holds the Guinness World Record for the largest single-author book signing in history, signing thou-sands of hardcover copies on July 3, 1998, at a major chain in Los Angeles. That year's tour included forty scheduled appearances, twenty-seven cities in twenty-eight days, both in the United States and Canada. He was also the first fiction author in history to sign at the Target store. If his name isn't familiar to you, you're not an *X-File, Star Wars,* or sci-fi fan.

According to *Publishers Weekly* in 2000, Borders and Barnes & Noble scheduled more than 23,000 events each year. The independents organized 400 more. That number has drastically declined.

To unite and excite the changing reader, bookstores added warm fuzzy reading spaces, plush sofas and chairs, and cappuccino bars. Some were quiet places right inside the adjoining Starbucks. They also hired customer service representatives (CSR) whose sole responsibility was the coordinated effort to bring authors and readers into their stores.

Daily calendars, large billboards touting the visiting author, multiple magazine and newspaper racks, music and computer software departments, creative writing classes, and programs devoted to genres like mystery or children, create a homey one-stop shopping environment that means more exposure for the author and more income to the seller.

What about the tour? The book tour requires a flexible day job, disposable income (spending dollars you can good-bye to), a loving and supportive family, groups of close friends (some of them writers), an ego made of Kryptonite, a smile and strong handshake, frequent flyers miles you've saved for years, and a strong marketing savvy. You're not in this business to make money. You're an author.

HINT: Ray Bradbury told the story about his marriage to his beautiful wife, Maggie, very early in his writing career. Mr. B. and Maggie were married in the Church of the Good Shepherd Episcopal in Los Angeles, CA on September 27, 1947. He had placed a few dollar bills in an envelope and, after the wedding ceremony, handed the envelope to the minister.

The reverend said, "I heard you're a writer."

Ray answered, "Yes, I am."

The minister handed the unopened envelope back to Ray saying, "Then you're going to need this more than I do."

Most large publishing houses, and there are only five left, will only book a six to eight city tour for a mid-list author. Their marketing budget averages $1,500 on a good day. They claim it's the law of diminishing returns for them financially.

How Do You Find Bookings?

In addition to the *Literary Market Place*, how do you find those stores that actively promote author signings? One source that has compiled a list of over 500 independent bookstores is Open Horizons, P. O. Box 2887, Taos, NM 87571. (505) 751-3398. John Kremer is a self-publishing guru. info@bookmarket.com www.bookmarket.com

What about your financial returns? Chapter One covered the basic questions of your business plan. They included:

- Who will buy the book?

- How do I position myself in the market to guarantee sales?
- How do I create a desire for this work?
- How do I sustain sales over a period of time?

When you position yourself in the market, you will make money. But it takes considerable time and effort on your part. Maximum exposure outside your local area is critical to hand-selling the book and creating name recognition. That's why you're doing the tour. Not for your first book, but those you'll write later.

Mid-list writers aren't going to get the big advance bucks, the dumps (those colorful cardboard stands advertising and holding your book), or the shelf space that Grisham, Patterson, and Koontz receive. You must be creative to enhance your share of the market sales to meet your business goals. Here are ideas that work:

- Get someone in the store to read your book. Most stores have an eye-level "recommended reading" shelf that will boost sales.
- When signing at an independent store, send them a poster for their window. When you leave after the event, offer to sign it for the store owner.
- Ask to be situated toward the front of the bookstore, near the entrance or a high foot traffic area.
- Even though you may have scheduled only an hour there, be prepared to stay until the last potential customer in your line has been greeted.
- Become your own sales person.
- When readers ask, and they will, "Who do you like to read?" have an author or their body of work in mind and answer readily.

- This helps the store sell additional titles.
- After the signing, autograph as much of the leftover stock as the store suggests. They place stickers that read "Signed Copy," or "Autographed First Editions," and place those in a special area in the store. Those books sell. Some distributors will not allow autographed books to be returned to the store, so hopefully consider those you signed—sold.
- If it's not a big chain that has their own printing department and makes professional posters in metal stands, provide the store with a photo of you and one of the front book jacket, or a poster you've produced.
- If it's a large store, provide duplicate signs to be strategically placed throughout the store.
- On the genre shelf turn at least one of your books "face out," a major plus because the cover is far more enviable than seeing the spine.
- In fact, when you go to any bookstore, whether you're there in an official capacity or not, "fix" your novel to achieve that look.
- On the signing table set one or more books upright.
- Carry several identical pens. If you've autographed them in black, the balance of the dedication and date, etc, needs to be in the same ink.
- If you're signing at a location other than a bookstore i.e., luncheon, conference, workshop, private home, designate someone to stand slightly behind you to accept the book, open it to the page you want to sign, and slide it under your hands. This gives you more time and freedom to talk with your buyer. You can look at your new fan and share more chat time rather

than thumbing through the front of the book for the signing page. It's smoother and less distraction for you both.

- Always be prepared. Carry books every time you leave the house.
- Wear comfortable shoes. Standing authors greet potential customers.
- Know where the restrooms are. If you're sitting down, customers will inevitably mistake you for the store's information person.
- Carry a camera. Take photos of yourself and your store contact. Put them in your gallery on the website, your blog and/or make a video.
- Autograph and mail the photo with your "thank you" note. That'll be your invitation to speak next year.
- On your first tour wear a name tag. This defines you as the author, not the employee.

HINT: My first signing was Valentine's Day 1998, at an independent store. I baked heart shaped cookies. You know, those packaged cookies that come in a roll? The four dozen fit nicely in a red, heart-shaped $.39 plastic bowl. Later, the bookstore owner recommended me for a paying job at the Learning Tree University. And she continued to hand-sell the novel after I left.

One often overlooked non-traditional book signing and selling market, especially for the mid-list author, is the library system.

Many libraries have developed year-round programs designed to bring more readers into their realm. Be prepared to donate one or two books to the library's inventory as a goodwill gesture. And, while the Friends of the Library will sell your book, expect to bring the books you will sell.

Negotiate in advance what percentage of the sale you'll donate to the Friends. Sixty for you and forty for the house is not unusual.

Mail them your press kit just as you would for a bookstore. If the library is near, drop off a poster they can use in the lobby to announce your appearance.

> **HINT:** Using a software program, I created bookmarks announcing the library program, included mailing labels for the area zip code from my master list, and delivered them. The librarian was pleasantly surprised with this idea. They gave a bookmark to everyone who rented a book and seemed interested in the program. Using our combined mailing lists, the library mailed more bookmarks, wrote a nice news release for the newspaper, and a reporter covered the event, which resulted in a front page article and photo afterward. The librarian thought the idea so unique, she reimbursed me the paper costs and now announces many of her programs in this manner. Where else can you buy advertising that cheap?

Book distributor Baker and Taylor has published state-by-state directories of libraries that offer author readings. This reference includes the library name, location, contact information and areas of interest. Contact the library marketing division at Baker and Taylor, 1120 Route 22 East, Bridgewater, New Jersey 08807; (800) 775-1500, (908) 218-0400 for a copy btinfo@btol.com www.btol.com

Many corporations and organizations will often pass on authors unless the event can benefit you and their store. In today's market, it's all bottom-line for everyone concerned in selling. Before scheduling the tour, consider these questions and have ready answers:

Develop a sales pitch.

- Can you sell books?
- What's your sound byte?
- What is your dowry?
- Do you have a large area mailing list?
- Is this your hometown?
- Can you and/or your publisher co-op a press release and advertising to bring readers into the store?
- Can you position yourself with a value-added promotion?
- Can you teach their creative writing class?
- Can you turn your product into a fundraiser?
- Can you develop a panel and bring in other authors in your genre?
- Do you know people with complementary products?
- Look to specialty groups according to their interests, careers, sex, lifestyle, race, creed, or political beliefs, if that will work with your product and your message.

A select number of large houses bring in the big authors and, rather than scheduling book tours, simply take the book buyers out to dinner with the author. The selling is left to the buyers. From the publishing standpoint, part of this is economics. Sometimes it's because the author can't speak in public, won't, or doesn't want to speak. How many top-ten perennial authors do you know who go on tour?

M. Scott Peck, author of *The Road Less Traveled* set a personal goal of one radio show a day as a critical part of his marketing plan. He conducted over 1,000 the first year, most from the comfort of his own home.

Events, whether major or minor, are part of the local outreach programs in every city. They bring readers into the stores. Don't be discouraged by the fact that more than fifty million Americans over the age of eight cannot read, and only one in seven of those numbers will ever enter a bookstore or library.

Make it your responsibility to increase both literacy and readership.

Offer to present your book for book clubs. Churches, schools, and private groups also conduct book reviews. And they buy books.

Should you speak at the chains or the independents? The answer is yes—to both. Many genres have specialty independent (indies) bookstores. The advantages are obvious. The insides have a dedicated client base, are locally owned and operated, and the owners read and hand-sell your book, matching your genre to their readers.

> **HINT:** Two independent bookstores posted my debut novel on their best sellers list the summer of 1998. Their customers believe and trust that the owners will match their reading interests with a new author. One independent places so much confidence in

> their reading recommendation that they guarantee a full refund if the buyer isn't completely satisfied with the title suggestion. The faithful mystery fan is the best.

While the major chains are gobbling up the indies, you must support the indies. They welcome you into their cozy reading rooms, get to know who you are, friendships develop, and they continue to follow your career and recommend you for other speaking opportunities. They have mailing lists and do newsletters—more good stuff for your press kit.

The mystery genre is fortunate to have a wonderful online resource with listings of all mystery bookstores, conferences, awards, magazines and newsletters, collectors, authors, fan clubs, mystery theater, party planners, and writer organizations in the WORLD. Visit http://www.mysteryreaders.org

> **HINT**: How do you find the bookstores interested in booking authors? Look at established author's websites under their event or schedule page. I put the name, address, and all contact information on mine. Feel free to steal it. Isn't the internet wonderful?

There are ways to reduce your costs. Before those dates are scheduled, make sure the book signings have ultimate value to you and to your fans. Ensure publicity, balloons, flyers, and media attendance. Mail out postcards or email messages to all those names on your mailing lists within three or four zip codes of the store location.

First class postcards are often less expensive to mail out than bulk mail rates. And you get address corrections from postcards free. Or email your notices saving a ton of time and expense.

Make a second set of those labels and send them to the bookstore for their newsletter mailing. Double and triple whammy your sales.

Bookwire.com is an on-line book site by R. R. Bowker. The *Calendar of Events* contains information about author appearances at bookstores, media interviews, and speaking engagements. Enter your event on-line in the "Calendar of Events" at http://www.bookwire.com/calendar.html

To list titles in *Books in Print*, contact Mary Hallock at R.R. Bowker. 630 Central Avenue, New Providence, NJ 07974. (888) 269-5372 ext. 0073 mary.hallock@bowker.com Writersclub.com hosts chat rooms where you can plug the tour.

Post your schedule and/or link your website to all organizations you've joined. Don't overlook the remote reader. Book-Talk founder David Knight found a market for this service, a 24-hour recorded book-discussion line, for those readers who can't get to signings. "It creates that bridge between the author and reader." This is an excellent resource for your publisher/or yourself to advertise your product. booktalk.com

When you're visiting a new town for any reason, identify and locate all the bookstores. Always drop by, offer to sign books, meet and greet the (CSR) Customer Service Representatives that book authors. And, in the case of the indies, meet the owners. Those stores reap the benefits of having autographed books, without the expense of having you there. Again, more sold books. They must get to know you because your success depends on it.

HINT: When I first wrote mysteries and was away from home, I always visited the locally-owned mystery stores. Sometimes I take cookies, a fresh press release, or offer to take the owners to lunch. Marketing is finding and nurturing long term relationships.

Develop sound bytes and create presentations that focus on a multitude of issues and concerns to local organizations like Rotary, Soroptimist, Kiwanis, Lions, Elks, Moose, and the Optimists. Join the Chamber of Commerce. They have a newsletter, hold weekly meetings, and possess a large mailing list of local retailers who are potential booksellers and buyers. People who belong to one group often belong to more. Those contacts extend your speaking opportunities, your networking, and your mailing list.

Don't forget seminars on cruise lines. Negotiate and you may receive the cruise free or at least at a greatly reduced rate.

Going to a spa? Offer to speak in exchange for room and board. Massage therapists barter. So can you.

Introduce yourself to all the book buyers at box stores like K-Mart, Costco, Sam's Club, and Wal-Mart, and work your way up the "food chain" to the regional purchaser for books. Locally, a few managers have purchasing power and most would welcome a non-traditional book signing. Ask, ask, ask. The hard work doesn't begin unless they say "no." The "yes" is easy. Remember that 85% of all books are sold through discount houses, price clubs, drug stores, and other non-bookstore climates. The danger here, though: they buy books at deeply discounted prices, i.e. up to 80% off the RETAIL price. And no checks arrive for more than 90 days thereafter.

Speaking of non-traditional markets, look for places where your book may be a hit:

- Try truck stops, convenience stores, car washes, and dealerships.
- What about professional places, like medical offices, hospital gift shops, cafeterias, museums, specialty stores, local schools, greeting card shops, pet stores, churches, strip retail stores, and malls?
- There's QVC, Home Shopping Network, television infomercials, internet writer's forums, and electronic bulletin boards.
- People who eat, buy books. Don't forget cafeterias, convenience stores, and restaurants.
- The world is on the move. Airline in-flight magazines, airport gift shops, car rental agencies, travel agencies, salons, and catalog sales. Take a book to the gift store at the hotel where you're staying. Find out who the buyers are and bombard them with your press.
- Find quiet places like libraries and coffee houses.
- Government agencies.
- Fun family events like street fairs, festivals, and trade shows. To reduce costs at these public events, try coopting with someone else on the price of a booth.
- Banks and savings and loans.
- Auto clubs.
- The postal service where your mailbox is located.
- Consider education a part of your contribution? Sponsor a community activity. Mentor a writing contest. Offer to teach classes in your field of expertise. Contact colleges and universities and propose to teach a class

or be a visiting instructor. Call the Learning Annexes. Their pay is minimal, but the contacts and the potential for future work is ideal.

- Contact independent organizations that have banded together to form their own brand. The Northern California Independent Booksellers Association (NCIBA), represents many bookstores throughout Northern California. The brand is *Book Sense*. They have buying power and book signing is a one-stop shopping opportunity. 651 Broadway, Sonoma, CA 95476. (415) 561-7686 http://www.nciba.com or http://www.bookweb.org/btw-topics/book-sense or info@nciba.com

- The American Booksellers Association, representing bookstores throughout the United States, is another. Contact them at 200 White Plains Road, Tarrytown, NY 10591. (800) 637-0037, (914) 591-2665 info@bookweb.org or http://www.bookweb.org

These groups associate themselves with knowledge of their products, passion about literacy, involvement in the community, and personalities that meet reader needs and bond the reader to the author. What else would you need?

When you're on the tour and budget dollars concern you, consider these cost reduction ideas:

- Sharing rooms
- Co-op a booth
- Getting reduced rates through AAA, AARP, etc.
- Using frequent flyer miles
- Staying with friends and family
- Calling airline brokers that buy blocks of seats at

greatly reduced rates

Regardless of the publisher's participation in your publicity program, you can do much on your own to increase your exposure. What better way to do this than a free story filler? This becomes part of your publicity package.

Press Release

After outlining the book tour, a simple, yet effective publicity method is the press release. You must have the answers to the following questions:

- When does the media want a press release?
- How should it look on paper?
- What information does the media want?
- What is the reader interested in?
- Can you solve a major problem?
- Can this release inform, inspire, entertain, or educate?
- What specific knowledge do you have above all others in your similar position?
- Where do I send it?
- How do I find the media sources?
- Do I need to hire a clipping service?

Let's face it; the media wants press releases because they need news. If you are announcing the release of your book, a speaking engagement in the area, an award you've won, a conference you're attending, a book signing, anywhere you want an audience, send out a press release.

A news release follows a business-like standard format, is double-spaced, generally contains less than 850 words, and is typed on plain white bond paper.

Start at the top of the page, write NEWS RELEASE. A few lines down, type "For Immediate Release" followed by the date. Some publicists suggest this line begin at the far left; others start at the far right, so either is acceptable.

Drop down a couple more lines and type CONTACT: followed by your or your agent's name and telephone number. Give daytime and evening numbers because presses run twenty-four hours a day. Add your address and email, too.

Drop several lines again and center a headline, preferably with an action verb: "Author wins Edgar Award." They may not use this headline, but it makes you look professional and gives the journalist an idea.

Now write the release. Double space your copy. The first paragraph contains all the basic information. It makes a statement, paints a picture of the who, what, when, where, and why. The second paragraph is the solution. The third and last is the summary.

These can be reduced to several critical points:

- The *who*? Begin with your name. . .
- Followed by an active verb like "offers,"wins,"reveals"
- The *what* target market? Secrets, tips, alternatives, guidelines, advertises
- The *when*? The reader will reap benefits after they read it
- The *where and why*? Calls the reader to action
- Closing with a sharp, crisp ending.

Subsequent paragraphs add information. But the first paragraph may be the only thing that the newspaper, magazine, or radio station has time and space to use, so don't waste it.

At the end, type "End." A row of hash marks like ######
will also substitute as the ending.

The releases should be sent to daily and weekly newspapers, local magazines, news radio and television, including cable stations nearest the event. Send them at least two weeks in advance.

Don't overlook church bulletins, trade magazines, and all organizations you belong to. Many have newsletters and magazines that reach their entire membership list. Those press releases should be sent sixty days ahead of the event, as most of these are published monthly. When in doubt, call. You don't want to miss a printing deadline.

The first time you prepare a news release, you're going to find it time-consuming. To identify the resources, the central library will have a reference section for sources like *Bacon's Magazine Directory*, *Bacon's Newspaper Directory*, and *Bacon's Newspaper and Television Directory.*

Write down the address and the editor's name and telephone number. Always call and verify the accuracy of all information printed anywhere. People are mobile in every industry. Writing is no exception.

You may wish to call in a week or so and follow up to see if more information is needed. If they ask you to resubmit, title the page, "Requested Information."

This publicity has a positive and a negative side. Many publications won't use the information until after it's stale, if at all. And they won't send you a clip for your records if they print it. On the other hand, when they print it, the value of the media does drive sales.

Clipping Services

Clipping services can be very expensive, and they won't always catch every word containing your name and book title. In addition to your own search every day, rely on friends, family, and the organizer where you're presenting. When you speak, ask the hostess for a copy of the clipping, especially when you're on the road and don't receive a daily paper. They generally have copies for you.

If you want a clipping service, maybe you're lucky enough to belong to a writing organization that has one. Those are much less costly than the major houses. Several sources include:

- Burrelle's Information Services is an international organization. Their headquarters is located at 75 East Northfield Road, Livingston, NJ 07039, info@ burrellesluce.com and http://www.burrellesluce.com
- GeoTel Corporation Newz Group has a clipping service covering nine states: Arkansas, Iowa, Kansas, Kentucky, Missouri, South Carolina, Texas, West Virginia, and Wyoming. Contact Doug Galaska at P. O. Box 873, Columbia, MO 65205, (800)474-1111 info@newzgroup.com or http://www.newzgroup.com
- Want to get on the top television interview shows but not sure how to find the contact person? For the most accurate listings of the major network shows, order *Harrison's Guide to the Top National TV Talk & Interview Shows from &* Bradley Communications Corporation, 390 Reed Rd, Boomall, PA 19008 (484)-477-4220 SteveHarrison.com

Can you do all this, write, and speak too? Sure you can—but do you want to? Let Chapter Six help you decide if your time and money are better spent hiring a professional.

CHAPTER 6

Whose Publicists are they Anyway?

There are three types of publicists: the one the publishing house assigns to you, the one you hire out of your own pocket, and you. Can you schedule everything on your wish list, write the next novel, prepare for all the events, and have a life? You will if you have budget restraints. Hopefully, there are options.

If you were fortunate enough to be published by a large house and given an astronomical promotional budget, we're very proud of you. All you have to do is provide that person with your calendar for the oncoming year so they can schedule dates around your life. May you be blessed that they return all your calls, care about you intensely, and get you on top TV shows. You're way ahead of the rest of us.

But, if you have a limited promotional budget from the house or no funds at all, you'll need to define your goals early and start saving your money.

How do you find these publicists?

Do your homework.
- Your agent and the publishing house publicist are good resources.

- Seek a referral from someone who already had a major publisher with an independent publicist. Ask who they would use if they had choices. Their reputation is important.
- Look for the publicist's name on the acknowledgment page of the author you most admire in your genre.
- Ask the author, if his/her publicist isn't listed.
- At writer's conferences drop in the press room and ask their opinions.
- Check out the *Literary Market Place*.
- When the author speaks at major functions, the publicist should be there. Find him or her and introduce yourself.
- Always have your business card and your sound byte ready.

Before contacting a publicist, consider your needs. What do you want from your career? Do you want to be rich, famous or simply move books?

What's your goal? Make the *New York Times* best seller list? Increase your status with your publishing house?

Do you need a full or part-time publicist?

Define the territory you wish to cover.

Time constraints should coincide with pub date. Minimally, publicists need a ninety-day lead time before the pub date in order to provide the highest exposure for your tour.

What is your budget? If the proposed costs are beyond your budget, save the publicist for their professional part, and you hire an admin to do the other tasks.

If you simply can't afford a publicist or want to do it entirely yourself, try the *Maximum Exposure Marketing System* from

MarketAbility, Inc. They will provide you with a loose-leaf workbook complete with fill-in-the-blank forms on all the topics you need to cover. 6061 N. Wayne Rd, Westland, MI 48185 (800) 123-4567 maximummarketing.com

On the other hand, if it's national publicity you seek, New York City or Los Angeles are the hubs that deliver the best results. On the west coast, one of the largest firms is Irwin Zucker's Promotion in Motion located at 714 N. Crescent Dr, Beverly Hills, CA 90210 bookpublicists.org. They've been in the promotion business for over fifty years and know everyone. (323) 461-3921. IrwinZuckerPR@aol.com

Book Blitz: Getting Your Book in the News: 60 Steps to a Best Seller (Paperback) by Barbara Gaughen and Ernest Weckbaugh is a highly recommended read for all authors who want to sell. For information on their firm, (323) 461-3921 www.bookpublicists.org

Brian Farrish Radio Promotions have extensive database lists. mike@radio-media.com (310) 998-8305

For the best and most comprehensive list of radio shows that do interviews, contact (my favorite) William Gordon of North Ridge Books. He provides his lists with updates on Word and Excel. P. O. Box 2832, Rancho Mirage, CA 92270 (949) 533-5106 info@nrbooks.com

Once you've selected a potential publicist:

- Send the publicist a galley copy, a press kit, and a brief letter of introduction, asking him/her to review the material and call you for an appointment if he/she is interested.
- Type up a marketing plan. Include things you'd "like" to do and places you'd like to speak. Be extravagant. The Tokyo Book Fair may be perfect for your product.

- When you first meet, take a copy of that plan.
- Is there a personality fit, and a common understanding regarding the size of the territory you wish to cover (your market focus)? Discuss fees based on your wish list. Don't faint when you hear the number. Remember you can negotiate anything, and under most circumstances, you can negotiate monthly or quarterly installments.

What are your goals? Schedule another meeting when you both have had time to review the plan against each of your goals. In subsequent conversations or meetings, talk about the media territory you hope to cover with the book and where you both agree the promotional focus should be.

What do you want him or her to do? Code each item according to whom you both agree can best schedule this event. "P" for publicist, "A" for the author, and "C" for the publishing house. This will ensure the best return for the money invested. Discuss the initial contract quote, downsizing it to fit your budget.

Can you afford it? Sign a contract with the publicist. Provide him/her with a copy of your calendar for the time period ahead so he/she will not schedule conflicts disrupting your home life. Knowing that you'll be on vacation in a certain state, however, may define additional speaking engagements there.

> **HINT**: My first publicist was recommended by a mystery author I greatly admire: Taylor Smith. I sent the publicist my book and a press kit. She read it and called me. We scheduled a face-to-face meeting. I

presented her with a twelve-page single-spaced wish list of everywhere I wanted to speak in 1998.

We perused the list, selecting which items I could do best. Then, based on her assets and view of the marketplace for my product, what she could do for me. And finally, what I should expect the publishing house to do. She developed a quote and sent me a contract.

That was the best promotional money I ever spent. Her name is Anita Halton in Laguna Beach, CA. Phone (949) 376-5780. ahapub@aol.com

Talking about money, let's talk costs. The hourly rate publicists charge ranges from $50 to $300. Sometimes you'll get a monthly quote, also known as a monthly retainer, payable through the life of the book tour. This is usually three to four months long. Most will charge you expenses, including telephone, Fax, copies, and postage. Ask for a monthly accounting. Decide how comfortable you feel, then insist on approving any singular expense above a certain dollar amount, like $50 or $100.

What can you do yourself? Don't pay publicist rates for tasks that you or someone you could hire at home would do at a lower hourly rate, i.e. answer fan mail, make travel arrangements, or manage your calendar. Save the professionals for the tough stuff, like helping you sell that book.

You can negotiate flat rates, daily rates, monthly retainers, costs plus, whatever. Remember to keep your eye on the budget dollars and define the highest result with the best publicist.

Relationships are very important. When the person is the

right one for you, you'll know it. As the book tour winds down, you'll feel a sense of loss for that constant contact. That's when you know you made the right decision.

In many ways, finding a publicist is like finding a literary agent. It's a marriage and like any marriage: some work, others don't. Good communication with that person, matching business styles, and being professional are imperatives. Does he or she return calls promptly and have ready answers to your questions? Is he or she accessible? Is he or she enthusiastic? What other services does your publicist offer? Does he or she offer tiered pricing? Is there a guaranteed campaign? Looking for some free publicity?

Google Book Partner Program is an online book marketing program designed to help publishers and authors promote their books by showing a limited number of pages at http://www.books.google.com/partner supportgoogle.com

Books in Print lists mystery and crime books written by SinC members that will be in print in the next calendar year. (758) 842-1325 admin@sistersincrime.org

It's almost time for your close up. Camera! Lights! Action! Let's get dressed.

CHAPTER 7

Dress to Sell

Dress to kill—well, at least dress to sell. First impressions are everything. What are you going to wear? Packing for the tour shouldn't mean a fancy and costly wardrobe, but remember you represent your body of work and how you want fans to respond and remember you.

Runs in your hose or holes in your socks? Always carry a spare pair. Dress like this is a special occasion, because, for you and the reader, it is. If you want the audience to remember something special about you, make it your signature.

Wear a hat when you don't get a chance to get your hair done. Keep your nails neat and attractive. That's what the fan sees when you are autographing their book.

HINT: Stan Kent writes erotic thrillers. His suits are straight from Seville Row. His hair is short and spiked with clear gel. His colorful British accent is a plus, and his charm cannot be ignored. His shoes are always shined, not scuffed. He carries an extra shirt and fresh tie.

That spaghetti sauce isn't particularly appealing when you're the after-luncheon speaker. Club soda is a good stain remover, but not always available or effective.

Ladies, leave that charm bracelet and things that dangle and clang at home. Jewelry or other accessories should not make noise or interfere with sound quality of the microphone. They also get caught in zippers, hair, and woven material like sweaters. On the radio, the earphones will mess your hair up ladies, so take a hat for later. On television, the mike is generally clipped to your shirt above the last button, or on the tie. The battery pack is looped over the waistband.

The important thing is to be honest with yourself and set the tone for what you want others to remember about you. The flight attendant will gladly take your jacket and hang it up. If the flight isn't loaded with hand-carry, you can also stow it in the overhead above your seat. If you're driving, put it on a padded hanger to reduce those sitting wrinkles.

And, my pet peeve for goodness sakes, please turn off your cell phone from the time you enter your program until you're totally away from the event site.

These are items to consider packing:

- Comfortable shoes because you're going to be standing and walking a lot.
- Take a spare pair.
- A small briefcase.
- Extra business cards.
- Your value-added items like postcards.
- At least one handout should have your website address or advertising on it.
- Several pens in the same color ink, in the event that one is lost or runs out of ink.

- Tissue-you never know.
- Extra bookmarks or handouts that you have developed as "point-of-purchase" items.
- A notepad. Invariably someone will ask you for something you don't have, like a date to do another appearance. Jot that information down and follow it up later.

How Do the Professionals Interview?

Before going on a particular television show look for these specifics:
- Watch that format and environment of the interview. Is the program a one-on-one or panel discussion? How many minutes will your segment run? Practice those very few minutes.
- Will you be seated next to the host or separated by a desk or other guests? What does the backdrop look like?
- Who is their target audience?
- See what works and doesn't work for others.
- Pants are recommended for ladies rather than a short mini skirt. Knees are not photogenic, even for Cindy Crawford and Sharon Stone.
- Turn off the sound and watch the interaction between the host and the guest-the non-verbal things.
- What do they wear? How do they sit? What does their body language suggest?
- What are the camera angles?
- Who does the guest look at?
- Where does the moderator sit in relationship to the

guest? Do you have a chair, a sofa, or a tall stool you'll have to climb up on?

- Is the guest chewing gum or playing with her hair?
- Is she adjusting a jacket that's too small or tugging at her skirt or pants? Maybe she's nervously crossing and uncrossing her legs, or worse, tapping or shaking a foot?
- Practice, practice, practice, to avoid these "tells." They distract the viewer and the host and make you a less desirable guest for a follow-up visit.
- Take the host a small gift, including your autographed book.
- Let's talk colors. White is the worst color on camera. Blue is the best. Jewel tone colors bring out the fleshy tone of your skin. Pastels wash you out. Solids are favored to patterns but develop your own style.

Watch late night shows and see what the hosts say about what their guests are wearing. You'll be surprised if you focus on this area of the interview.

Dressing to be Remembered?

If you 're a Hawaiian shirt, "please-look-at-me" kind of guy, then just do it. Maybe you're James Bond and like tuxedo jackets for day wear. Just do it. Don't forget, it's your style, and you're entitled to set the tone for your career.

CHAPTER 8

Your Business Plan. . . Staying Alive, Staying Alive

One component of your business plan is increasing your market share and sustaining sales.

How Do You Sustain Sales When Your Fifteen Minutes of Fame Has Passed?

Lectures and speaking engagements can continue long after the tour is complete.

- Find one or more subjects that you are an expert on and develop a lecture or a series.
- Tie in tapes from previous radio and/or television events to enhance the value of your product. Package them to sell.
- Network during each event with an eye toward the next appearance.
- Write a syndicated column in any publication, no matter how small. Do this for free, for the exposure. Start with one, establish a track record and extend your market into other areas.

- Send postcards that reach potential customers for nearly half the price of preparing and sending letter mail.
- Get testimonials and/or product endorsements. Use the ones you like to upgrade press kits, make flyers, and create ads.
- Author Gerald Schiller created a colorful coupon. For anyone who purchased an autographed copy of *The Dog That Belonged to No One,* he'd give them one-dollar cash. Time sensitive to the conference, they were stuffed in tote bags and on the author's "goodie" table.
- Contact *Novelists, Inc.* Members are all professional writers. Don't forget to mention your work. P.O. Box 54, Hartland, MI 48353 ninc@varney.com or http://ninc.com
- Teach at a senior center, an adult education group, or start a creative writing class of your own.
- At the library, stroll through the *Literary Marketplace, Encyclopedia of Associations,* and *National Trade and Professional Associations.* No matter what your book is about, there's a world of book buyers waiting for you to find them. You might advertise in a newsletter or magazine, speak at trade meetings, conventions, or customize a course and offer to teach.
- Share a booth at the local trade fair.
- Who has the most popular live radio talk show? Get booked. You have something for everyone.
- Jeffrey Lant wrote *How to Earn a Whole Lot More Than a $1,000,000 a Year Writing, Selling and Commissioning How-To Information.*

- Give autographed copies of your novel to the gatekeepers (secretaries, assistants). If they read and like it, they can help you get past that locked door.
- Find addresses of celebrities who might be interested in your product and mail them copies of the book. *The Address Book* and *The Corporate Address Book* by Michael Levine have almost 10,000 listings of the famous and the infamous. Think that Reverend Billy Graham might be interested in giving you a review for your project? His address is there along with that of several convicted murderers on death row.
- *Book Page* is a monthly review that reaches hundreds of U.S. bookstores. There's an excellent opportunity, if you purchase an ad, to reach 2,500 bookstores and 3,000 libraries. Contact: Julia Steele at ProMotion,Inc. 2143 Belcourt Avenue, Nashville, TN 37212. (615) 292-8926 https://bookpage.com/content/contact-us
- Attend book fairs for your particular genre, i.e. new age, astrology, romance, western round-up days, Christian, literacy events, annual library book sales, Star Trek, nudists, whatever.
- Plan on attending the American Booksellers Association Convention, now called Book Expo.
- Attend the library convention, both regionally and national.
- Encourage other speakers or conference organizers to sell your books if you can't attend. Work out a sharing plan on the sales.
- Ask for help. "Ask" being the key word. Ask for publicity, speaking engagements, writing opportunities,

whatever you want. You will get lots of "no's" along the way. The truly successful people in this world will help others. You will pass others on your way to success.
- Is your product conducive to having a corporate or organization sponsor? That will certainly bring in more money for advertising and offer greater distribution.

Are There Other Ideas to Consider?

When speaking and selling ask yourself the following:
- Does this audience have money to purchase my book?
- Do they want my value-added products?
- Do I offer enough variety to achieve balance in those sales? How many people will attend?
- Will they buy additional copies as gifts? What is the organization about? What is its mission statement?
- Have I personalized my presentation to bond with them?
- Will I have all the answers to their questions? Or know where to refer them for those answers?
- Will my product solve their problems, enhance their lives, help them achieve their goals, make a positive statement?
- Is there such a great need for my product that they'll be willing to pay whatever it takes?

Once you've joined organizations and are published, work to develop co-op ads. For example, Sisters-in-Crime does two each year: one in spring and one in winter for *Publishers Weekly*. This gives you an opportunity to be seen by over

150,000 subscribers for only a few bucks an ad. You can't buy an advertisement at that rate in any magazine in America.

Don't forget audio and video packaging. Audio books constitute a large market for book sales. Seventy-three percent of their customer base listens to books during their long commutes to and from work. Nonfiction, entertainment, and self-help are the most popular topics. Audio Publishers Association reports that listeners select their choices based on the subject matter, then the author's reputation, and the recognition of the title. This method also helps you reach sight-impaired readers and seniors as well. Not to mention that huge audience of families who live in their RV and travel America.

During your first year on tour, select three or four conferences to attend. Develop value-added products. You will complete an application, and send in your registration fee. Also include your press kit, refer them to your website, and ask to be assigned to a panel or teach your own class. Ask the organizers if you can send tools ahead.

HINT: At Bouchercon, the world mystery conference, I mailed postcards that showcased the book jacket along with one of my bookmarks to the organizers. Someone stuffed them into the totes that every attendee received. Out of over 250 authors there, only two had thought ahead, and I was one of them. Thirty-five hundred new fans and readers then knew about my book.

Take all your promos for the "goody" table. It's usually messy, and you have to stop by and straighten it up throughout the conference until they are gone. But it's worth it if you have an eye-catching item.

Hand out more promos at the door where you are speaking and take extras for the book signing table and the book sales room.

Get a blow-up of your jacket cover made into a poster. Usually a 17" x 12" will fit flat in the bottom of your luggage. Prop the poster up everywhere you are.

The cost less than five dollars each for four-color and are excellent marketing tools.

Set a goal to book a certain number of radio interviews every day. M. Scott Peck conducted over 1,000 in his first year. Most can be taped and performed from your home, a hotel room or your mobile telephone. Those are known as "phoners."

Want a Real Low Budget Tour?

Obtain a list of radio stations from the local libraries in cities where you know your book will be in stores. Contact the radio stations and determine if they have talk shows. Identify the producers and their guidelines for submission.

Generally, a one-page letter (or press release) to the producer with a press kit and the twenty questions and answer sheet inside is sufficient. Don't present yourself merely as an author. Focus on the fact that you're an expert on a specific topic. Hopefully, you will make it timely and provocative.

Follow up with a phone call. When you're booked, be certain that you're upbeat, articulate, entertaining, and knowledgeable about the topic. Also, close out the world around you: the television, other telephones ringing, the children or pets. You will need total focus and be relaxed. Stress or being rushed is a death knell to your success.

Name recognition equals book sales. The *Chicken Soup* guys say, "Get on as many magazine covers as possible."

> **HINT:** Mid-list authors have a tougher time with this one. In 1998, for me, that was July's *NEXT Magazine* cover. But several scrapbooks containing press clippings are comforting memories.

Ready for Your Close Up?

To schedule your television appearances, list yourself in *Radio/ TV Interview Report* Bradley Communications Corporation, (610) 259-0707 custservice@freepublicity.com They print 35 issues a year and will write your ad copy free and submit it to you for final approval. Since 1986, they have placed over 10,000 authors on the air. Mary Duffy, a producer for the *Montel Williams Show* was quoting as saying, "I love it! I use it all the time."

CHAPTER 9

The Inner Sanctum of the Internet

The internet has evolved technically to become the writer's best resource (dollar-for-dollar) for book reviews, interviews, book sales, and news releases. In the year 2010, it is conservatively estimated that 250,000,000 were on the net. It helps if you have a ten-year-old at home who can help you with this technology. Now that amount numbers in the billions.

Today, you can conduct business on everything that touches your life. Rent an apartment, price an automobile, find a job, buy or sell stock, or bid on auction items. You can find a word in a dictionary. And locate a high school friend or a former lover. You only need to capture 25,000 of those buyers to reach the best seller list.

The explosion of modern technology would not be complete without developing its unique share of weirdoes, crazies, fanatics, crooks, frauds, liars, cheats, and sickos, in addition to good folks. You'll learn words like "lurkers, berserkers, flaming, and junk mail." The internet is faceless, and anonymity sometimes breeds contempt. Like a thief in the night, one mistake, and your financial, emotional, or physical life can be destroyed. Guard your assets, private numbers, and access codes. Enter this community with caution and respect.

If you're internet impaired, find yourself a webmaster;

someone who knows how to build and maintain a site for you. Setting up a website takes skill. Don't be embarrassed if these geniuses are under the age of ten.

> **HINT:** At my first signing, Raul Melendez entered my life. He built and maintained my website for years until his own writing career took off. Thank you, Mel, from the bottom of my life.

If you have talent, time, and the interest, develop your own. You'll need to use HTML. There are several web writer programs, like Composer that comes with Netscape Communicator. You might download a copy of TUCOWS. It's easy to learn and not expensive if you decide to purchase it. Others include Claris Home Page, Microsoft Front Page, Adobe's Page Mill, and HomeSite 2.5. Because the industry is booming, please check your software stores before making a final decision. There's no way a book like this can keep up with all the innovative changes occurring in technology today.

When setting up your site, create one with its own identity. A "domain name," as it's called, is important.

- It protects your company or trademark and when others are searching for you, it makes finding you easier.
- It means you're big enough to have a domain name.
- You can switch between Internet Service Providers (ISP's) more easily.
- Make it short and sweet so it fits on your business card and is memorable.

To reserve your domain name, try <u>Domain.com</u>. Check InterNic Registration Services, <u>domreg@internic.net</u> (703) 742-4777. Go Daddy is another popular domain site. <u>godaddy.com</u> And I'm sure there are hundreds of others.

Plan your page in advance. First, identify what you wish to accomplish with the site, setting goals for yourself. Next, think about a name for your URL, Uniform Resource Locator, that identifies each website. Make it individual so others can find you. Then design it following these ideas:

- A fast-loading graphic. For many PC owners, time is money.
- A table of contents or menu bar.
- Your email address as a link with a message from you to your fans.
- Links to other sites, including Amazon.com and/or Barnes & Noble.com.
- A counter may be important for the hit totals if you're into numbers. However, the hits are there for the world to see. Would you be embarrassed if there are no hits?
- Press Releases including works in progress, appearance schedule, your bio, and photos of you and/or the book jacket cover.
- A guest book is a great way to develop an email list.
- Excerpts, especially the complete first chapters, are very effective on the net.
- Avoid huge graphics, borders, or busy backgrounds.
- Don't try fancy fonts. Go with the proven.
- Be flexible as you may change it often.

Some ISP's (Internet Service Providers) will give you a free home page if you sign up for their internet access service.

However, they may attach ads on your site, so it isn't entirely "free." Shop around before you engage someone to develop this important tool for you.

The key to the success of your site is keeping the personal message and appearance schedule current.

Is Everybody Else Out There Doing This Too?

You bet. With over one hundred fifty million websites, how can you garner your share of hits and buys?

- Place your site on every piece of paper that leaves your hands. Forty percent of all business cards and stationery now feature an email address.
- Mention this in every presentation.
- It should be listed in all your books and placed on all flyers, brochures, or ads.
- Offer to "speak" on-line with popular zines and mention it during the "interview."
- Place it in major web directories and list it on internet malls.
- Find special database sites and post it; i.e., if you have a bookstore, contact the ABA Bookstores at http://www.bookweb.org
- Cross link your site with those of the organizations you joined.
- When you're in chat rooms, mention your site.
- Do mass mailings online. Postmaster Direct is the email list rental product of the Postmaster Network and has more than five million people on mailing lists. Contact them at https://www.postmasterdirect.com

- Rent out your own mailing list to Postmaster Direct if you have at least 5,000 names.
- For more online activity whether you're interviewing, selling or wanting the book reviewed:
- *Bookwire.com* offers all levels of membership, a professionally written, unbiased book review that can be used in all of your book promotion activities.
- The Book Report Network reviews books and conducts author interviews. http://www.bookreporter.com
- http://www.blackwriters.org is the website address for the African-American Online Writers Guild, the premier community for black writers.
- If you write poetry, www.borderlands.org This is one of Texas' finest reviewers of poetry.
- If you want a copy of your favorite movie script, stop by info@scriptcity.com
- Novel Advice is devoted to the craft of writing. Try http://www.noveladvice.com where you'll find a critique forum for your work, resource forums, and a writers' chat forum to discuss the finer points of writing. aj@noveladvice.com
- In 1993, David Knight founded BookTalk, a 24-hour recorded book discussion line. Publishers pay fixed rates a month to record their authors. If the recordings stay on longer, the costs vary. The author prepares a script, does the recording and BookTalk does the taping. Hits on this line result in greater exposure and sales potential. booktalk.com
- Pat Holt is the former book review editor and critic for the San Francisco Chronic/e. Her Holt Uncensored is an online book news column. Her commentary

includes industry issues, author interviews, book reviews, and hot tips. To subscribe go to: http://www. holtuncensored.com or p.holtiz@comcast.net

- To reach the Canadian book market, bookstores, libraries, schools, and professional groups, contact Association of Canadian Publishers, 174 Spadina Ave, Toronto, Ontario MST 2CZ (416) 487-6116. admin@canbook. org or http://www.publishers.ca. This association also publishes the Directory of Canadian Media. acp.ca

- If your book has college level potential, don't overlook this $8.15 billion market. Thousands of college store managers and buyers attend an annual conference. Contact the National Association of College Stores, 500 E. Lorain Street, Oberlin, OH 44074-1294. (800) 622-7498 info@nacs.org or http://www.nacs.org

- Subscribe to an internet list for booksellers called Publishers Daily. This site contains current information and seeks blurbs on new books that will be posted.

- If your book has gossip appeal, try: http://www. eonline.com Editors might feature it on *E! Online*. Doesn't hurt to try.

- The Publishers Marketing Association's info@pma-on-line.org. They'll respond to questions you may have on marketing.

- Bonnie Mercure's Guide to Writers' Markets lists writing opportunities. http://www.dowse.com

- The Short Mystery Fiction Society, http://www.thewindjammer.com provides a way to see your work on screen and has been in business since 1996. shortmystery.blogspot.com It's an opportunity to be discovered by other zines. The prospects here are endless.

Riding the Amazon Wave

How do you catch the Amazon.com wave and sell your novel? Amazon began in 1995, and now boasts more than six billion customers in over five hundred countries who buy books from its website for both the print and the e-books. Here are a few ideas to enhance your sales:

- You can provide Amazon with cover art, a synopsis of the work, the introduction, whatever you can to achieve the highest exposure on the net.
- There are online interviews that help introduce you to your potential audience. Reach them at www.amazon.com/books
- Take advantage of developing "keywords" so your work can be associated with as many topics as possible.
- Amazon.com has many editors who will review the book. From the homepage, pull down the "subject" menu and locate the correct editor. Send that person a copy of your book to Amazon.com. Include other reviews that you may have to increase the editor's interest in reviewing it for you.
- Encourage your reviewers to add their opinions to the buyer's page once your book has been accepted. This generates excitement and may help the sales remain high.
- If you're self-published or from a small press with distribution concerns, contact Amazon. They have an Advantage Program that enables them to carry a small amount of stock to assure their 24-hour shipment

guarantee. They will require a discount and 55% is the recommended figure, plus free shipping. www.amazon.com/advantage

- If you list your website on the Amazon's listing, that may drive potential buyers to you. That's how you find readers and buyers interested in your product and add to your mailing list.
- If your topic is similar to a more popular book that has a huge marketing budget and publishing house, shirttail on the hits to their page. Read that book. Do a review and at the bottom, add something like "if you like this book, try . . ." And list the title of your book. People will find you who might otherwise not know you.

You can start your own discussion group on Yahoo. Find a subject matter that's related to your genre and contact staff at http://www.groups.yahoo.com/neo. One club will spawn another as more discussion groups interface with yours. Those are readers out there. Find them and help them find you.

Organized in 2003, you might be an author in the Worlds Without Borders' chat room. Be part of the international exchange. area. http://es.paltalk.com. Readers have an opportunity to ask questions and receive an instant reply.

To market your book on the web, you need to get into the big bookselling databases. The biggest book database is probably *Books in Print*, from R. R. Bowker, the firm that handles the ISBN (or international standard book number) system for all books published in the U.S. A book buyer will probably want to use smaller databases developed by the major wholesalers, like Ingram and Baker & Taylor, and chains like Barnes

& Noble. Amazon Books and Nautilus buy their books from Ingram and use the Ingram database so you get multiple listings. There are other sites like Koen, BookPeople, Bookazine, and Alamo; while England has Book Shop and Turnaround, Marginal in Canada, and Bulldog in Australia.

John Kremer has developed a database, *Top 700 Independent Bookstores,* order at http://www.bookmarket.com or call (641) 472-6130. This list features the largest bookstores that work with authors and buys books from small independent book publishers. Contact them and go through the listing process. Finally, set up your website to link to all the bookselling sites.

Is your "marketing brain" kicking in? Good. Add your ideas to those in the next chapter.

CHAPTER 10

More Marketing Mania

Every year tens of millions of manuscripts are sent to top five publishing houses. Of those numbers, less than 60,000 per quarter are accepted for publication.

If your project is nonfiction, you have a better than average opportunity to become a chosen one, because two-thirds of all manuscripts published are non-fiction. And you only need to sell 25,000 hardback copies a week to become a best seller or so we're told.

Did You Know There Are Ten Seasons of Book Selling?

- Valentine's Day
- Easter
- Mother's Day and Father's Day
- Graduation
- Summer
- Back-to-School
- Halloween
- Autumn
- Thanksgiving
- Christmas

If the genre fits any of those ten seasons, plan the marketing to enhance sales during that period of time by tie-ins to special interest groups.

- Seniors
- Baby Boomers
- Generation X's
- Children and Grandchildren
- Teenagers
- Women
- Men
- Hispanics
- African-Americans
- Businesses
- Computer and Technical
- Cooking
- Fitness
- Gardening and Home Repair
- Religious and Spiritual
- Self-help
- Travel and Leisure
- Trendy
- Poetry
- Specialty Fields like
    - Mystery
    - Sci-fi and Fantasy
    - Biography and Autobiography
    - Romance
    - Mainstream

Did You Think About This?

To promote your books to schools, stores, libraries, and the media, associate your promotion with the more than 4,000 special days that are celebrated each year. Many of these may be obscure, but could be a great tie-in with your novel. Contact Open Horizons, P. O. Box 2887, Taos, NM 87571 (575) 751-3398 info@bookmarket.com or get a copy of *Celebrate Today!* at bookstores or direct from johnkremer@bookmarket.com. It features thousands of events. Their data file (only from Open Horizons) contains thousands more.

- Send holiday cards to all the people and organizations that you have worked with throughout the year. You want them to remember you. Not for this book; but for the next one, and the one after that.
- Send a theme card, like a birthday, Valentine Day, July 4th, to introduce your new novel. Booksellers always receive the typical things: flyers and brochures. Work outside the box and do something different.
- Adopt a charity or library and donate a specific amount; i.e., one dollar a book, or net proceeds, from the sale of each book.
- Book distributor Baker & Taylor developed a state-by-state directory of libraries that encourages author readings. (800) 775-1800. publiclibrary.btol.com

HINT: After my five-part series, "So You Want to Get Published," appeared in the *Desert Woman,* a local women's newspaper, I received numerous calls from readers who read only one part and needed the others. I bound the entire series and offered it as a value-added product: three dollars when it was mailed, or two dollars as a handout.

- Use a money-back guarantee for books and tapes that you sell directly to the public. History indicates that the longer the guarantee, the fewer the returns.
- Make a list of all the products that can be "spun-off" your book. All the value-added items will include tapes, handouts, and goodies like T-shirts, caps, or greeting cards.
- Excerpts from your novel make great sales teasers. Type it up, bind it and give it away at selected venues.
- Many authors print the first chapter of their next book in the back of their current book. If your chapter ending hook is there, they'll want more and wait impatiently for the next one.
- In your newsletter, try selling ads to vendors that have a tie-in to your product.
- The Jenkins Group, Inc. formed a special sales division that helps authors and small press publishers find new markets. 1129 Woodmere Avenue, Suite B, Traverse City, Michigan 49686. (231) 933-0445. publish@ jenkinsgroupinc.com
- If you self-published or have a small press, don't get too discouraged about distribution. Contact Ingram's submission information hotline: (615) 213-6803. Staff will ask for four free copies of your book, plus additional documents you'll find listed in detail at http://www.ingramcontent.com. When you have everything in order, contact Phil Frazer, Publisher Relations Supervisor, 1 Ingram Boulevard, LaVergne, TN 37086-3629; (615) 287-5369, (800) 937-8100, ext. 5369. pubrel@ingrambook.com or http://www.ingram-book.com. When they've accepted your book and you

want to know the stock levels, call (800) 937-0995; for actual sales figures, note the ISBN and call the Ingram Stock Status Line at (615) 213-6803 and enter the ISBN at the prompt.

- Sell on television. QVC and Home Shopping Network sell books. They are particularly interested in theme books. Contact their producer and get a list of future programming themes. Make it work for you. QVC Network (888) 345-5788, Follow the product submittal guidelines http://www.qvcproductsearch.com. If you have questions or comments, contact Vendor Relations at (888) NEW-ITEM or vendor_relations@qvc.com
- Home Shopping Network: start the vendor product submission process by contacting customer service at (800) 284-5757 and online at HSN.com
- Create your own blog that keeps your reader in your writing and touring life. Many authors have a newsletter instead of a website. Others have both.
- *Brands and Their Companies, A Gale Trade Names Directory* is an excellent resource for promotional tie-ins for your novel. Worldcat.org for a catalog
- If your genre might interest the law enforcement community, contact Calibre Press, Inc. at P O Box 3476, Glen Ellyn, Ill 60135, (941)-0900 questions@calibrepress.com or www.calibrepress.com. They publish *Street Survival Newsline,* an email newsletter that reaches 600,000 law enforcement professionals in the United States. Their subscribers print out the ezine, share it with other officers, post it on bulletin boards at the station, and often quote from them in other meetings. The publisher claims an additional 250,000

readers from this broadcasting approach.

- United Airlines has two in-flight magazines: *Hemispheres* and *Rhapsody*. <u>unitedmags@ink-global.com</u>
- American Airlines' magazine *InFlight* began in 1994. <u>http://magazines.aa.com</u>
- Now, almost airline and hotel chain has a magazine. One of them, Holiday Inn Express, has an in-room magazine *NAVIGATOR* which is a prime place to promote your book. InterContinental Hotels Group, 3 Ravinia Drive, Suite 100, Atlanta, GA 30346-2149. (770) 604-2000.
- Does your product include sharp tips, clever strategies, make readers feel better? Try the *Bottom Line Publications*. With over a million readers don't overlook this market. Contact Bottom Line Publications Editorial/Corporate Offices, 281 Tresser Boulevard, 8th Floor, Stamford, CT 06901-3246. (203) 973-5900, <u>http://www.bottomlineinc.com</u>. They'll direct you to the department that matches your message.
- Create "continuous loop" videotape of reviews and promos for trade shows and bookstores.
- Are you sick? Know someone who is? Distribute "waiting room" copies all the way to the cemetery. And there too, if your product is a natural tie-in.
- *Chicken Soup, Dummies, Goosebumps, Kiplinger,* and *One Minute Manager* are examples of brand name success stories. Add your own to this impressive list.
- If you're promoting a cause, co-op with them for sales if they distribute and/or advertise your product.
- Free, local newspapers and publications are found in newsstands or restaurants throughout your

community. They are additional sources for interviews with you and about your book.

- Create that market by having someone read your book and do a review.
- Local "throw-away" papers need filler articles, especially when they don't have to pay a reporter for it. Both you and the publisher have a win-win here.
- Write an article or series of articles. At the end of each article add something like, ". . . is the author of. . ."
- Never overlook an opportunity to write down the title of your current work.
- Never miss an opportunity to "say" the name of your book – at least three times.
- The Lifestyle editor of your local paper may be more interested in you and your book than the book review editor. Your book is an extension of you. You are an inspiration to readers and, hopefully, you are the expert on your subject.
- Libraries usually honor requests from their patrons. Have your friends and family drop notes in the suggestion boxes requesting your book.

HINT: One local library had two copies of my book and developed a long waiting list. Someone rented one copy and refused to return it, paying the library full price for it. The librarian called and ordered several more books.

My bookmarks were in high demand. I often handed them out at airports, on airplanes, and in public places all over the world. People see them and make a comment. I give them one indicating I've written a book and if they like mysteries, they might think about ordering a copy. It helps tremendously when your companion says, "She's the author. It's a really good read."

- If you own a retail store or restaurant, or have friends who do, set up a "business card fishbowl" and offer a book as a weekly or monthly drawing. This is an excellent way to build up your mailing list.
- Never overlook an opportunity to barter. It's still big business.
- Scott Flanders, past president of *Macmillan Computer Publishing* and currently President, Chief Executive Officer and a member of the Board of Directors of Freedom Communications has been quoted, "We say that there are two successful books on the subject: The first one out and the best one." In your case, try to be both.
- Price your seminar and workshops to include copies of the book for each attendee.

Publishers Weekly plans issues well in advance and, as you may know, focuses on specific concepts. One week may be children, another religion, yet another romance or mystery. Check PW's site at www.publishersweekly.com to determine what the upcoming issues will cover. If you have an idea for an article or want to pitch a story, 360 Park Avenue South, New York, New York 10010; (646) 746-6758.

Probably one of the boldest and most successful marketing coups of 1999, belonged to mystery author Lisa Scottoline. She posted a draft version of her first chapter to her website, then invited the "hits" to try their hands editing it.

The press, including *The Wall Street Journal* and *The New York Times*, picked it up, which prompted hundreds more "wanna be" editors to log on to her site.

It'd be interesting to know, in the end, how many "editors" plunked down the $20 to buy her hardback to see if their edits were taken to heart. Way to go!

If you find something that really works for you-keep doing it again and again. You may re-write, re-title, or develop a new idea for distributing the product. Just do it. Set yourself a marketing goal each day to take action, even if it's just writing a letter, making a few calls, or doing one radio interview. It doesn't take time; it takes effort. But it's worth all this to keep your book alive for years.

CHAPTER 11

And Now for the Real Goodies

We've put together a huge list of sites that, (as of publication dates are accurate) and will promote your book. Some are free and others charge.

- http://www.kindlenationdaily.com/ wide readership reaches daily; expensive to participate with.
- http://www.worldliterarycafe.com This site is driven by Facebook, Blogging, and Twitter. I added my blog to promote *A Guide to Puppy Love; Beginner Breeding*. I do not use Twitter, nor do I care to start. Each individual Facebook user must sign up for themselves. Personal profile and pages were not accepted.
  - o Helpful resources: We've got you covered with resources for editing, cover artists, small press, helpful tips and tricks and much more. The Author Toolkit is a compilation of resources. Download the WLC Author Toolkit free of charge. This resource will be updated often.
- http://www.bargainbooksy.com/sell-more-books/ This site lists e-books ranging from .99¢ to $5.00 only. There is a cost to list and prices vary depending on the genre. My book, A Puppy Love Guide; About the Labrador Retriever was added for $25.

- http://www.icravefreebies.com/contact/ This site is only for free promotions but has a wide audience.
- http://bargainebookhunter.com/feature-your-book/ accepts low priced books; entered *A Puppy Love Day; Tips for Bringing Your New Puppy Home*. Their criteria to post is that the book needs to be 100 pages minimum.
- http://www.freebookdude.com Only lists free books; a wide range of readership.
- http://blog.booksontheknob.org/about-this-blog-and-contact-info I set up a discount promotion of this site. Through KDP I marked down two of our books for a week and sent them links for them to be featured; free promotion was successful and brought new readers to my other books. Win-win.
- http://addictedtoebooks.com this site requires a minimum of 8 Amazon stars to list a book. First, set up an account and once the account is approved will post your book(s) with specific discounted prices and rates.
- http://www.smashwords.com This link must be downloaded only by the author. It's difficult to load the cover and text, but there's a broad audience so stick with the rejection until the book is accepted.
- http://www.snickslist.com Prices are cheap, but the e-book must be free on Amazon. Reaches tens of thousands of people weekly.
- http://bestindiebooks.com/ This is a very easy site to use, very inexpensive with a wide audience.
- https://www.draft2digital.com/ Each author must submit their own work, and the site is very easy to navigate. Highly recommend.

- http://www.indiesunlimited.com/freebie-Friday.com
  This is a valuable site; packed with tons of information.
  They have a print book special to upload books, but
  the books must be priced below $15 to enroll.
- http://choosybookworm.com/author/ Sign up for
  a newsletter that costs between $25 and $70. But it
  currently reaches 60,000 people daily.
- http://ereadernewstoday.com/ is expensive, but may be
  worth the expense.
- http://home.bookbub.com/home/ is very expensive,
  but may be worth the expense.
- http://thefussylibrarian.com/for-authors/ has nominal
  fees, but the book needs 10 four or five-star ratings on
  Amazon before posting.
- http://digitalbookstoday.com has inexpensive trial
  periods for banners and other promotions. But they do
  have limited free promotions.
- http://www.peoplereads.com/ minimal price to sign
  for this site. But you have must have 10 Amazon
  reviews first.
- http://www.fkbookstandtips.com Must have a minimum of four-star ratings on Amazon.
- http://bookgorilla.com/ Subscribe but have to set up an
  Amazon author page to use this site.
- http://indiebookoftheday.com/authors/free-on-kindle-
  listing/ Books must be free to post on this site. Easy to
  use for a giveaway.
- http://www.ebooklister.net/submit.php is a free and
  easy site to use, books must be $2.99 or less and have
  min. of 3.5 stars.
- http://www.daily-free-ebooks.com/suggest-free-ebook/

This site scrolls Amazon for free and .99 books; they chose books to post on the site.

- http://www.dailycheapreads.com/your-two-cents-worth/ This site scrolls Amazon for free and very inexpensive books; they chose books to post on the site.
- http://www.manybooks.net Has a huge following. The cost is $25 for inclusion on the site. Requirements include a deep discounted book or free book. Must have at least 10 reviews and no less than 4 stars on Amazon.
- http://www.authormarketingclub.com/members/author-services/ This is a very helpful site. Filled with many links to help make a book professional. Has video links, links to book designers, and so much more.
- http://www.bookgoodies.com/contact-us/authors-tell-us-about-your-book/ this is individual author based. Each author must set this up for themselves. There are a lot of questions to fill in, but it is worth the time to do. The viewership is huge.
- http://www.awesomegang.com excellent site to post free or for $10. Fill out feature spot for a day. Do a free author profile page for extra publicity.

And if you give up writing altogether or want to dump all those unsold books you bought from your vanity press that is in your garage, here's one last idea, and I hope you never have to use it:

- Sellbackyourbook.com will give you an instant price to buy your book(s). But the total value must exceed $5 for all books you list.

This is a compilation of sites for promoting your book. It is worth your time to venture down the internet rabbit hole and discover which sites fit your needs:

http://www.goodkindles.net/p/submit-your-book.html
http://www.storyfinds.com/promotions-for-authors
http://www.bookdealhunter.com/submit-free-book
http://www.digitalbooktoday.com
http://www.ebookshabit.com/for-authors
http://www.ereaderperks.com/authors/
http://www.thefrugalreader.wufoo.com
http://www.freeebooksdaily.com/p/contact.html
http://www.flurriesofwords.blogspot.com/p/book-advertising.html
http://www.freediscountedbooks.com/99-cent-sales/
http://www.bookcanyon.com
http://www.kindlemojo.com
http://www.ebookdealoftheday.co.uk
http://www.onehundredfreebooks.com
http://www.iloveebooks.com
http://www.sweetiespicks.com
http://www.jungledealandsteals.com
http://www.kornerkonnection.com
http://www.pixelscroll.com
http://www.slashedreads.com
http//:freebookshub.com
http://www.everythingbooksandauthors.com
http://www.thedailybookworm.com
http://www.bookfreebies.com
http://www.fictionhideaway.com

http://www.hunt4freebies.com
http://www.ereadergirl.com
http://www.greatbooksgreatdeals.com
http://www.super-e-books.com
http://www.bookangel.co.uk
http://www.igniteyourbook.com
http://www.clickreading.com
http://www.feedyourreader.com
http://www.readcheaply.com
http://www.themidlist.com
http://www.readingdeals.com
http://www.bookpinning.com
http://www.ebookisland.com
http://www.ebooksoda.com
http://www.ereadercafe.com
http://www.ebookbooster.com
http://www.free-bookz.com
http://www.indiebookpromo.com
http://www.masqueradecrew.com
http://www.trainingauthors.com/booklemur
http://www.contentmo.com/99-book-promo/
http://www.sweetfreebooks.com
http://www.booksends.com
http://www.ebookarrow.com
http://www.booksbutterfly.com
http://www.bookhippo.com
https://www.facebook.com/groups/444695995585913/
http://www.submityourbooks.com/free/
http://www.crossreads.com
http://www.christiankindlenews.com
http://www.faithfulreads.com

http://usawrites4kids.drury.edu/
http://ereadernewstoday.com
http://www.thefussylibrarian.com
http://bookgoodies.com/contact-us/authors-tell-us-about
-your-book/
http://Pretty-Hot.com
http://bookreadermagazine.com
http://discountbookman.com
http://mybookplace.net
http://www.readwriteclub.com
http://authormarketingclub.com
http://wantonreads.com
http://myadultplace.net
http://www.justkindlebooks.com
http://freediscountedbooks.com
http://fkbt.com

CHAPTER 12

A Strong Marketing Message from Virginia Clark

Self-promotion of your published work is essential to the success of sales. You need to schedule time daily to establish your online presence. You need to follow up with your posts and messages in a timely manner. You do not need to be highly skilled in mastering your own online marketing program. With the rise and evolution of social media, the digital platforms are more streamlined; entering data is easier now than ever before.

Find out which sites are most effective in reaching your target audience. It is better to focus your attention on platforms that help you maximize your marketing goals than to try to be involved with so many sites that you've spread yourself too thin. You want quality over quantity in order to maintain the online relationships you've developed. Find what works best for you, stick with those sites, post intermittent, and engaging information, and be certain your posts reflect the professional image you wish to portray. Consistency is the key to successful online marketing.

Facebook is the market leader in social networking and in 2016 was the first social network to surpass 1 billion monthly active registered accounts. Your online presence on Facebook is essential towards branding yourself. Design a professional

Facebook page; leave your personal page separate. Your professional image should be engaging and honest so you attain regular followers that will, in turn, share your information with others in their network and help you grow your client base. Post your unique Facebook link to like-minded pages to further grow your audience. "follow" and "like" as many related sites as possible to continually expand your reach. An affordable feature for consideration is placing Facebook ads; they are inexpensive and allow you to target specific groups of people and grow your fan base which can result in sales. As you continue to develop your online presence through Blogging, LinkedIn, YouTube, Google +, or any other sites, be certain to update your Facebook page with the information so you remain current for your followers.

Installing https://apps.facebook.com/authorapp/ on your page is a great way to give your followers an overview of your publications. The easy-to-install app allows you to add details, engage in conversation, and list upcoming events for users to see. If your books are listed on Amazon, entering the ISBN or AISN is all it takes to get you started.

LinkedIn has become the most prevalent resource for professional networking. It makes good business sense to establish your profile on this site where over 300 million people engage monthly. This networking does operate differently than Facebook so be sure you know the differences between the two before you begin to establish connections. On LinkedIn, not all people want to network with people they are unfamiliar with. On Facebook, everyone "likes" and "follows" anyone regardless if they are familiar or not. While you may be excited to set up your new account and meet new people, it is best to grow your connections based on people you already know.

LinkedIn connects you to your base connections using your email address book. Allow your base of contacts to potentially grow your account naturally when your contacts share your information with their own connections. The gradual growth will increase your visibility. It is best to let each potential connection know how you found them and why you want to connect with them.

The first impression people will get of you is when your profile is viewed on LinkedIn. Building a professional and appealing profile will prove invaluable in meeting new people. Your profile should include professional looking head-shot; dress for success and look your best. Provide as much detailed information as you can without droning on and on and appearing boastful; brand yourself and be informative with a brief, attention-grabbing focal point. Including personal recommendations is helpful. Be sure you come across as a professional and avoid posts that appear to be spam or advertising. This will not help gain popularity amongst your connections. Signing up with groups related to your target audience will help broaden your connections; engaging in group conversations is an excellent way to meet new people. Keep your page up to date with your latest accomplishments and information so you remain interesting.

Blogging is another highly effective tool you must add to your marketing arsenal. More than 200 million blogs exist due to the online marketing explosion. The top ranked free blogging platforms are WordPress, Blogger, and Tumblr. I, personally, have been on Blogger for 10 years with great success. Blogging is one of the most successful tools to generate new leads that convert into sales. Not all platforms are created equal so you need to take a look at the top blog sites to determine which one will offer you the best opportunity for growth, exposure, and generation of revenue based on your target audience. You need to take the time to create an inviting blog; have a visually colorful theme and be imaginative to capture your audience. It takes just three seconds for a blog visitor to decide to connect with you or not. Too much information will create boredom, and too little information will prove useless. Find a comfortable medium to achieve success. Once you have developed a Blog you feel comfortable with, share your unique URL on your other social networking sites. Just like LinkedIn, you want to connect with other like-minded blogs and groups to grow your fan base. Blogging platforms are easy to use and any amateur can look professional with practice and patience.

As you become an experienced Blogger, get creative with your site and add widgets, also called gadgets. They are applications that can enhance your blog; a few examples of gadgets include adding a section allowing readers to subscribe to your blog, direct linking to your other interactive social media applications and a counter to see how many people visit your blog. There are thousands of gadgets to choose from and the list is continuously growing. The "help" section of your blogging platform can assist with adding gadgets to your site. If your Blog is Google based, like Blogger, you can apply for AdSense. This is a way to monetize your site with pay-per-click ads. If you have a large following and an interactive Blog, your application for AdSense might be accepted.

Another platform you can use to drive traffic to your Blog is Pinterest. It is becoming an increasingly popular site where people go to read articles of interest. Pinterest is much more than just recipe and craft ideas. Visit http://blog.wishpond. com/post/63664550828/9-ways-to-use-pinterest-to-drive-traffic-to-your-blog to learn how you can use Pinterest to broaden your audience.

Finally, remember to keep your blog up to date to keep your visitors returning on a regular basis.

With over four billion views daily, another marketing platform to consider is developing your own YouTube channel. My own YouTube channel has been quite successful and I attribute my creative use of YouTube as one of my more successful sales vehicles. Entrepreneurs and businesses using videos to create exposure are five times more likely to reach new customers. A successful video can generate sales, and monetization of your product is your end goal so why not venture into creating your own channel to promote your product? YouTube is easy to use social video networking site and the best part is if you do not like how your presentation turned out, you can delete and start over. With cell phone camera technology giving us a high-quality video, you can upload your work directly to your channel. You want your presentation to be professional so be certain you look your best, check your background so you do not have anything captured on the video that takes away from your presentation, speak clearly and distinctly without sounding rehearsed, and be clever. A lengthy or boring video will not be viewed. Once you get comfortable with making YouTube videos, share your links on your other social platforms. Like all social sites, people will not know your online presence exists if you do not share your link.

Google + is a site worth noticing. It has gained in popularity and is one not to ignore if you intend to enhance your marketing profile. Over 250 million users have already made this site an essential part of their social media campaign. You must have a Gmail account to participate with Google +.

The greatest benefit of using this platform is the major role it plays in SEO, search engine optimization. The more you post using your account, the higher your site is ranked thus making is easier to locate your online presence by people searching specific keywords. The higher your ranking results in higher click-through rates. I find this to be my favored site for marketing in conjunction with my Blogger account. Once I publish a post on Blogger, it automatically loads to Google +. To date I have 975,000 followers on Google +; this is a testament to how successful the combination works.

When setting up your Google + "About" page you want to include specific keywords that are relevant to your page. This will assist searchers in locating you. This is the page where you can detail your product and yourself to maximize your SEO. You can also include links to specific pages so be sure to include your other social media links on this page. When designing your page, you should use bullets in your description to create an easy to read list of information.

Using Google + is easy and fun to use. The success of your site will be a direct result of the conversations you engage in, the relevant groups you join, and the people you have in added to your Google "Circles." This unique feature allows users to categorize different people in specific groups making it easy to post relevant content to a direct audience. It is also easy to follow content from others that you find relevant and interesting. Using "Circles" will help you grow a local, national, and international fan base quickly.

Google + continues to evolve and new features are updated with regularity. Be sure to take advantage of the new additions to this platform so you remain on the cutting edge of social networking sophistication.

If real-time marketing excites you, then you want to take a look and Twitter. Acting like a micro-blog, people sending tweets (messages) are limited to 140 characters per message. Your tweets can include links to websites, blogs, documents, pictures, and videos. The information you share with your followers can be re-tweeted which furthers your communications and brings new followers. When selecting your account name and images, be sure you remain consistent with your other online presences to identify your brand. Visit Twitter to learn how to utilize their multiple offerings to your maximum benefit.

A valuable tool that you must have for marketing your book is setting up your Amazon Author profile page. This site is easy to use and allows you to share information about you and your works. Once your page is set up, you will get a unique URL that will take readers directly to your page. Once there, they can read your synopsis and purchase your book with just a few clicks. This URL needs to be placed on every social networking site you have established. It is the easiest, most streamlined way to get the reader to purchase your book. To get started: https://authorcentral.amazon.com

As the internet continues to expand, new platforms will continue to emerge. While highlighting the most popular interactive social platforms in this chapter, there are still many more options available. You need to decide which sites will help you achieve your promotional goals. Once you have set up your sites, you need to routinely visit those sites and keep your material fresh and exciting. It is common for people to jump on board with too many platforms and not keep them up-to-date and once your pages fall to the wayside, you'll have to work even more diligently to recapture your audience. Start small and grow as you go.

While we have discussed how you can use the internet to market your book, we've not touched based on a few things that are more conventional, and often overlooked in this digital age.

- Order business cards; don't go for the least expensive cards to save a few dollars. You want your business card to contain your contact information and your main online presence site, such as your Blog address. Your business card is your personal reflection. You want to give your card to people and they say "nice card" and keep it. A cheap card is likely to get thrown away; forgotten in a split second. Make your card memorable, and you'll be memorable. There are many online sites that make customizing your business card a cinch. My preferred sites are Vistaprint.com and Overnightprints.com. Both sites produce affordable, high-quality material with fast shipping. If you subscribe to eBates.com you'll earn cash back on your purchases; the site is free to join and thousands of merchants engage in rebates through this site.

- Stand out from the crowd, and be creative with printed goods that reflect your brand. For example, I make customized bookmarks that identify my brand and material. It is clever to give a free bookmark with each book sold. You can be assured the bookmark will be used again and again, and the reader is more likely to remember you. Place your Amazon Author URL on your bookmark so the reader will remember to visit your page and see any new information or new books you have available. Browse the online printing shops and find an item that is cost effective and allows you to give added value to your product.

- Word of mouth: the oldest form of advertising. Get people excited about your book, get them talking. In turn, do the same for any author friends you have built a relationship with through your social marketing. Ask those who purchased your book to give you a review; post the reviews on your Blog. Don't be shy; ask for an Amazon star rating and a review for your book. Boosting sales is the end game, so get the conversation started.

So, there you have it. Did you notice that Virginia kept using the YOU word? YOU are the conductor of your sales--not your publisher no matter how your book is printed. Only the top five houses will give you major marketing money, and it's going to take money to make money in sales.

We've shared our victories and our stories with you. Life is a learning experience. And learning is a daily event. If you have any clever marketing ideas that you'd like to share with others, please write us. If you tried something and fell flat on your face, tell us that story, too. We all need humor in our lives.

The road to publication is riddled with rejection. The path to sales, marketing, and promotion is a mystical puzzle. We believe the gift of sharing is very important. That's why we updated this book from the earlier award-winning version: Power Marketing your Novel. Who knows? You and your book title may be among those quoted in the next edition of this book.

Did you read the paragraphs above? We just gave you a shameless opportunity to promote yourself and your book in the next edition-for free. Have you learned anything about promoting and marketing yet? So power up your life and let us hear from you.

Joyce Spizer Foy, Senior Editor;

A Vegas Publisher

Joyce investigated cases involving millionaires, movie stars, and mobsters during her 37 years as a private investigator. She'd work in 11 states before retiring to the Palm Springs area and began her writing career. Armed with her Ph.D. in marketing and an interest in writing, she met such notable teachers as Ray Bradbury, Rod Thorp, James Frey, and Charles Schultz. Eventually, she completed the Harbor Pointe Mystery Series, a trilogy fictionalizing several of her own real-life cases.

Joyce has written, co-written, or ghostwritten more than 30 more books. Her first play, Valley Confidential was nominated in 12 categories for the 2005 Desert Stars. *Power Marketing Your Novel* won the IRWIN 2000 award in 2000. *Only Make Believe* (the life story of MGM sensation, Howard Keel) won the Hollywood Book Festival award in 2007. In 2000, Congresswoman Mary Bono gave her a Woman of Distinction award. In 2003, the *Desert Post Weekly* named her one of the Top 25 Women in the Coachella Valley to Watch. Along with Emmy-award winner, David Holman, they own Hollywood East Productions. They've written several screenplays that are in development. A life-long Dallas Cowboy fan, she helped get former Cowboy #70 Rayfield Wright's authorized biography *Wright Up Front* in print.

With his father, she wrote former Cowboy #80 Tony Hill's book published in fall 2009—*From Selma to the Super Bowl.* This is an updated edition of her award-winning marketing book, *Power Marketing Your Novel.* In addition to touring and teaching creative writing around the U.S., Joyce has several feature films and TV shows in development. In Spring 2015, Joyce was hired as Senior Editor and Acquisitions Manager for A Vegas Publisher, LLC. She now resides in Texas and belongs to Book Publicists of Southern California, IBPA, and SPAWN.

Virginia Clark, Junior Editor;

A Vegas Publisher

Virginia comes to A Vegas Publisher with over 25 years of diverse entrepreneurial experience. She owned/partnered in three successful businesses in Buffalo, New York prior to relocating in Henderson, Nevada in 2012. "I wore many hats during those years of owning and operating businesses and have acquired numerous skills that have been proven valuable as a Junior Editor with A Vegas Publisher."

Currently, Virginia is a licensed breeder of German shepherd puppies. With over 10 years of breeding experience, she is now an author of five published works. The first book, *A Guide to Puppy Love; Beginner Breeding* was released in 2015. She penned her second book, *A Puppy Love Day; Tips for Bringing a New Puppy Home.* She is compiling *The Puppy Love Series,* featuring the top ten most popular dogs in America according to the American Kennel Association. Currently in publication: *A Puppy Love Guide: About the Labrador Retriever, Tips for Bringing your Lab Puppy Home, and Doggone Delicious*

Recipes; A Puppy Love Guide: About the German Shepherd, Tips for Bringing your GSD Puppy Home, and Doggone Delicious Recipes; and A Puppy Love Guide: About the Golden Retriever, Tips for Bringing your Golden Puppy Home, and Doggone Delicious Recipes. "The most exciting part of being a Junior Editor is meeting new authors and helping edit their books for publication. I am an avid reader and enjoy the opportunity to read and help sculpt the manuscripts with the authors. I bring ingenuity to the table and thinking outside the box is my forte."

At the time of this publication Virginia Clark's first book, *A Guide to Puppy Love: Beginner Breeding* has been selected as a **Book Excellence Award Finalist** in the category of Animals and Pets. Hundreds of entries from around the world were submitted and her publication was selected for its high quality writing, design and market appeal. According to Virginia Clark "It pays to work diligently on your manuscript and to follow the marketing and promotional strategies in *Blitz Your Book to a Best Seller 21st Century.* Not only did I co-author the book with Joyce Spizer Foy, I applied the advice in the book to my own work and am now a proud and accomplished award winning author."

Visit the Library at A Vegas Publisher to purchase our publications directly: http://vegaspublisher.com/our-library/ Or Visit Amazon.com:

From Gumshoe to Cyber Sleuth, By Debbra Macdonald and Joyce Foy: https://www.amazon.com/Gumshoe-Cyber-Sleuth-Debbra-Macdonald-ebook/dp/B01ACLWQIU

Canadian Debbra Macdonald and Texan Joyce Foy have written the most comprehensive investigation manual for all of North America. Private eyes for more than 60+ years, these authors share their experiences in this A to U (Accidental Death and Asset Recovery to Undercover) in this manual designed to educate, inform, and entertain students, professors, librarians, and readers. It's a career guide for those looking for an exciting, sometimes dangerous, but high-paying job. Along the way, Macdonald and Foy have infused what otherwise might be a dull primer into fun and fact-filled stories of real cases they investigated. In the field of investigations -- Hollywood's "CSI" investigator carries a flashlight. Macdonald and Foy are the real investigators. They turn on the lights for you.

Sargent's Lady, By Judith Fabris:

https://www.amazon.com/Sargents-Lady-Judith-Fabris-ebook/dp/B01ABCBJ9M/
https://www.amazon.com/Sargents-Lady-Judith-Fabris/dp/0996843728/

Peter Wells discovers an old portrait in a Washington, D.C. antique store that he believes has not only been painted by

John Singer Sargent, but the Victorian lady's delicate features so intrigue him that he offers to buy it. The antique dealer refuses to sell the painting until it's authenticated. Thus, Peter begins a quest to learn more about this breathtaking beauty. Is this the face of someone he recognizes? SARGENT'S LADY is a story of love, sacrifice, and survival from the late 1800's - 1950's throughout the United States and Europe. After a clandestine love affair in Paris, Maud Driscoll, a Boston debutante, finds herself alone and pregnant, only to learn the baby's father has been murdered. As an aspiring young artist, Maud is forced by Victorian convention to relinquish her baby at birth. She continues studying and painting until the outbreak of the Great War when she returns to the United States. Several years later, Maud marries a prominent Boston scion but discovers her marriage a farce. Not wanting to face any public humiliation or gossip, she returns to Europe, this time to Italy. The subsequent years bring her worldwide fame through her artwork. She finds love and marries a baron. At the onset of WWII, the Nazis commandeer their home, destroying all the vineyards, and the winery. Maud and her husband, Giovanni, work as servants to survive the shattering onslaught. They stay alive, dreaming they can begin a new life in California. Post-war, Maud's life takes a dramatic turn. She finds her son and discovers he married the daughter of her best friend. The families unite in love and in common interests as they plant vineyards, and build a winery. Will history repeat itself?

The Puppy Love Series, by Virginia Clark:
https://www.amazon.com/author/-virginiaclark